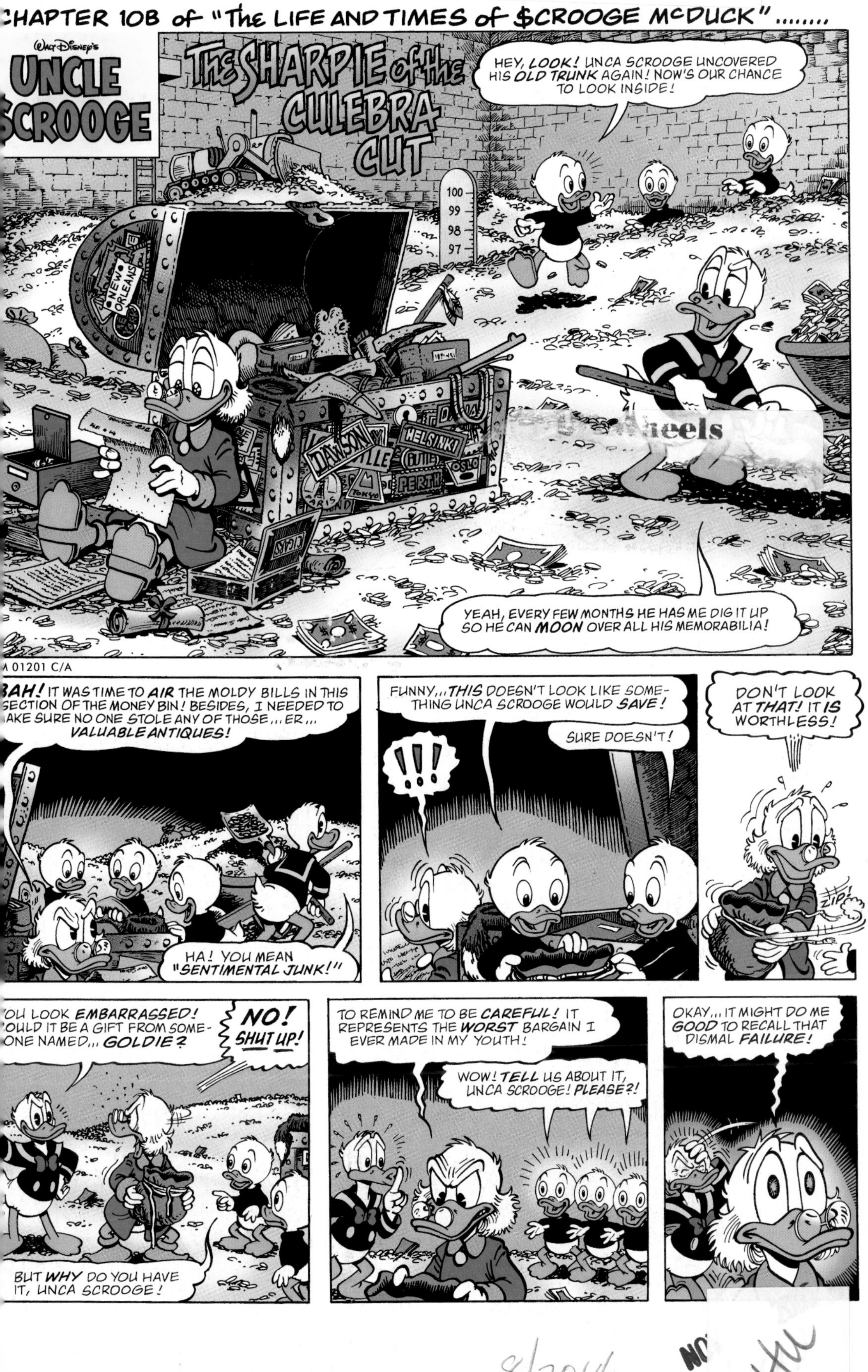
CHAPTER 10B of "THE LIFE AND TIMES of $CROOGE McDUCK"........
WALT DISNEY'S
UNCLE SCROOGE
THE SHARPIE of the CULEBRA CUT
HEY, LOOK! UNCA SCROOGE UNCOVERED HIS OLD TRUNK AGAIN! NOW'S OUR CHANCE TO LOOK INSIDE!
YEAH, EVERY FEW MONTHS HE HAS ME DIG IT UP SO HE CAN MOON OVER ALL HIS MEMORABILIA!
NEW ORLEANS
DAWSON
HELSINKI
OSLO
PERTH
TOKYO
PARIS
100
99
98
97
M 01201 C/A
BAH! IT WAS TIME TO AIR THE MOLDY BILLS IN THIS SECTION OF THE MONEY BIN! BESIDES, I NEEDED TO MAKE SURE NO ONE STOLE ANY OF THOSE... ER... VALUABLE ANTIQUES!
HA! YOU MEAN "SENTIMENTAL JUNK!"
FUNNY... THIS DOESN'T LOOK LIKE SOMETHING UNCA SCROOGE WOULD SAVE!
SURE DOESN'T!
!!!
DON'T LOOK AT THAT! IT IS WORTHLESS!
ZIP!
YOU LOOK EMBARRASSED! COULD IT BE A GIFT FROM SOMEONE NAMED... GOLDIE?
NO! SHUT UP!
BUT WHY DO YOU HAVE IT, UNCA SCROOGE!
TO REMIND ME TO BE CAREFUL! IT REPRESENTS THE WORST BARGAIN I EVER MADE IN MY YOUTH!
WOW! TELL US ABOUT IT, UNCA SCROOGE! PLEASE?!
OKAY... IT MIGHT DO ME GOOD TO RECALL THAT DISMAL FAILURE!

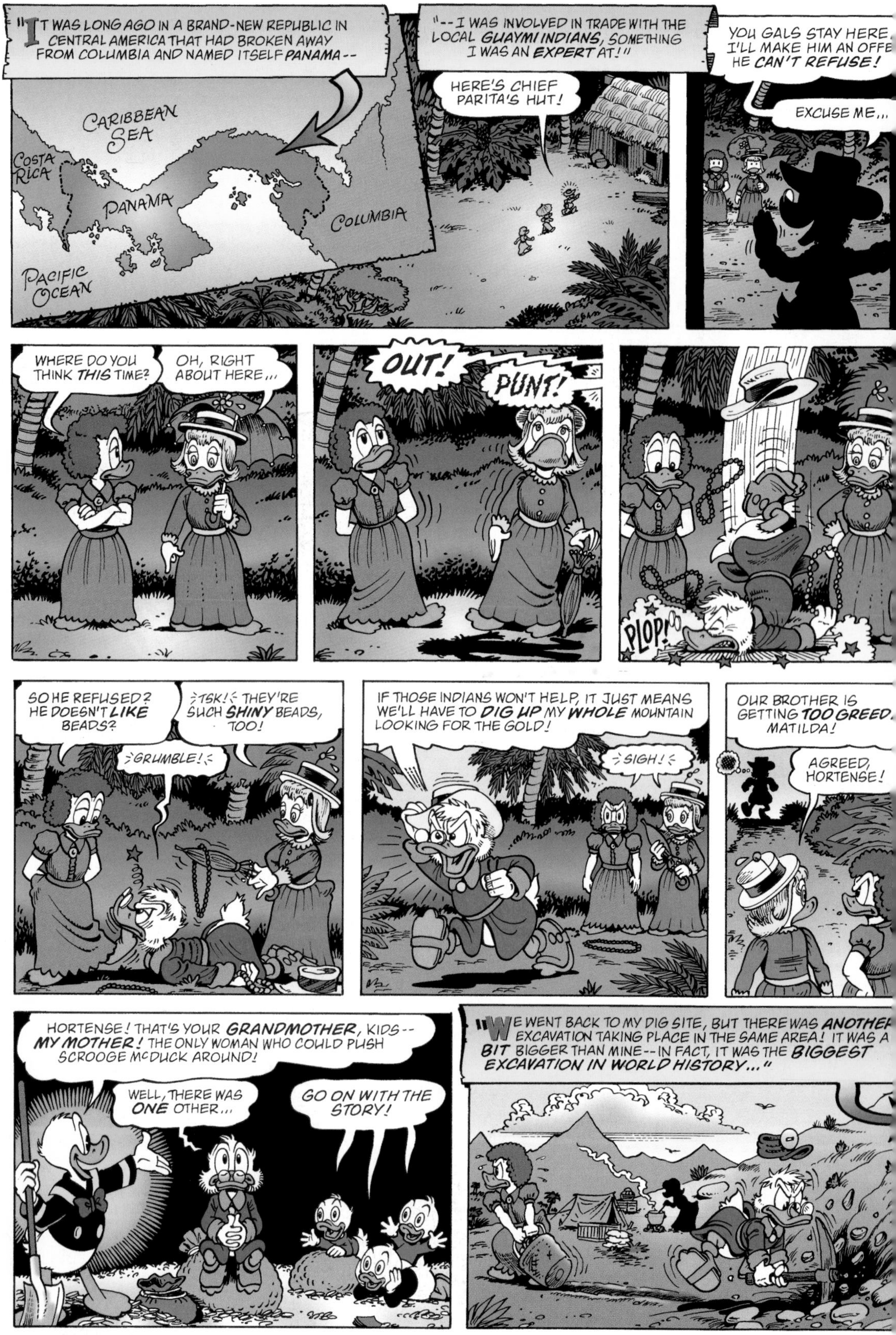

"IT WAS LONG AGO IN A BRAND-NEW REPUBLIC IN CENTRAL AMERICA THAT HAD BROKEN AWAY FROM COLUMBIA AND NAMED ITSELF PANAMA--
CARIBBEAN SEA
COSTA RICA
PANAMA
COLUMBIA
PACIFIC OCEAN
"--I WAS INVOLVED IN TRADE WITH THE LOCAL GUAYMI INDIANS, SOMETHING I WAS AN EXPERT AT!"
HERE'S CHIEF PARITA'S HUT!
YOU GALS STAY HERE. I'LL MAKE HIM AN OFFE HE CAN'T REFUSE!
EXCUSE ME...
WHERE DO YOU THINK THIS TIME?
OH, RIGHT ABOUT HERE...
OUT!
PUNT!
PLOP!
SO HE REFUSED? HE DOESN'T LIKE BEADS?
TSK! THEY'RE SUCH SHINY BEADS, TOO!
GRUMBLE!
IF THOSE INDIANS WON'T HELP, IT JUST MEANS WE'LL HAVE TO DIG UP MY WHOLE MOUNTAIN LOOKING FOR THE GOLD!
SIGH!
OUR BROTHER IS GETTING TOO GREED MATILDA!
AGREED, HORTENSE!
HORTENSE! THAT'S YOUR GRANDMOTHER, KIDS-- MY MOTHER! THE ONLY WOMAN WHO COULD PUSH SCROOGE McDUCK AROUND!
WELL, THERE WAS ONE OTHER...
GO ON WITH THE STORY!
"WE WENT BACK TO MY DIG SITE, BUT THERE WAS ANOTHER EXCAVATION TAKING PLACE IN THE SAME AREA! IT WAS A BIT BIGGER THAN MINE--IN FACT, IT WAS THE BIGGEST EXCAVATION IN WORLD HISTORY..."

356740398 36037

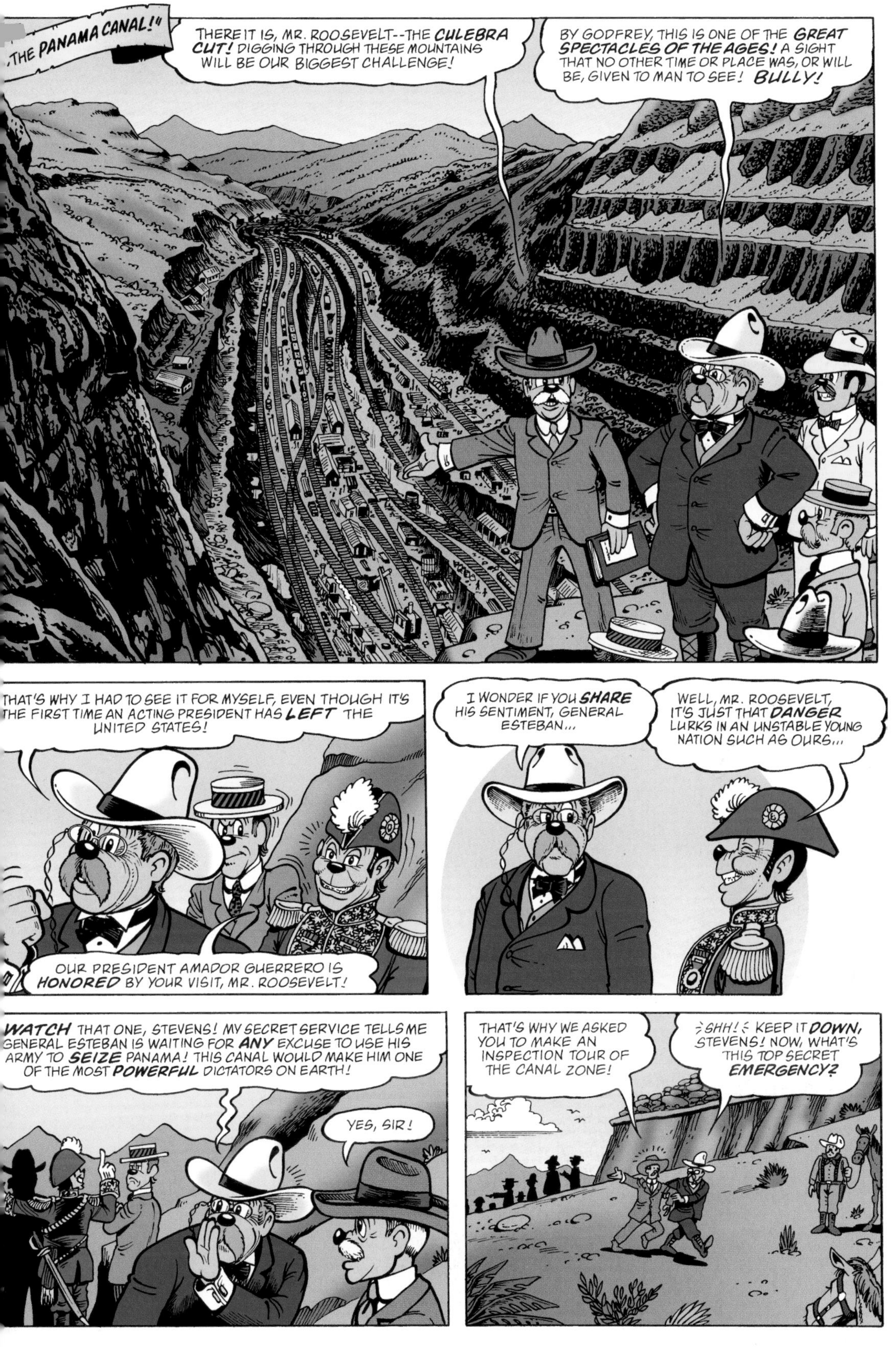
"THE PANAMA CANAL!"
THERE IT IS, MR. ROOSEVELT--THE CULEBRA CUT! DIGGING THROUGH THESE MOUNTAINS WILL BE OUR BIGGEST CHALLENGE!
BY GODFREY, THIS IS ONE OF THE GREAT SPECTACLES OF THE AGES! A SIGHT THAT NO OTHER TIME OR PLACE WAS, OR WILL BE, GIVEN TO MAN TO SEE! BULLY!
THAT'S WHY I HAD TO SEE IT FOR MYSELF, EVEN THOUGH IT'S THE FIRST TIME AN ACTING PRESIDENT HAS LEFT THE UNITED STATES!
OUR PRESIDENT AMADOR GUERRERO IS HONORED BY YOUR VISIT, MR. ROOSEVELT!
I WONDER IF YOU SHARE HIS SENTIMENT, GENERAL ESTEBAN...
WELL, MR. ROOSEVELT, IT'S JUST THAT DANGER LURKS IN AN UNSTABLE YOUNG NATION SUCH AS OURS...
WATCH THAT ONE, STEVENS! MY SECRET SERVICE TELLS ME GENERAL ESTEBAN IS WAITING FOR ANY EXCUSE TO USE HIS ARMY TO SEIZE PANAMA! THIS CANAL WOULD MAKE HIM ONE OF THE MOST POWERFUL DICTATORS ON EARTH!
YES, SIR!
THAT'S WHY WE ASKED YOU TO MAKE AN INSPECTION TOUR OF THE CANAL ZONE!
SHH! KEEP IT DOWN, STEVENS! NOW, WHAT'S THIS TOP SECRET EMERGENCY?

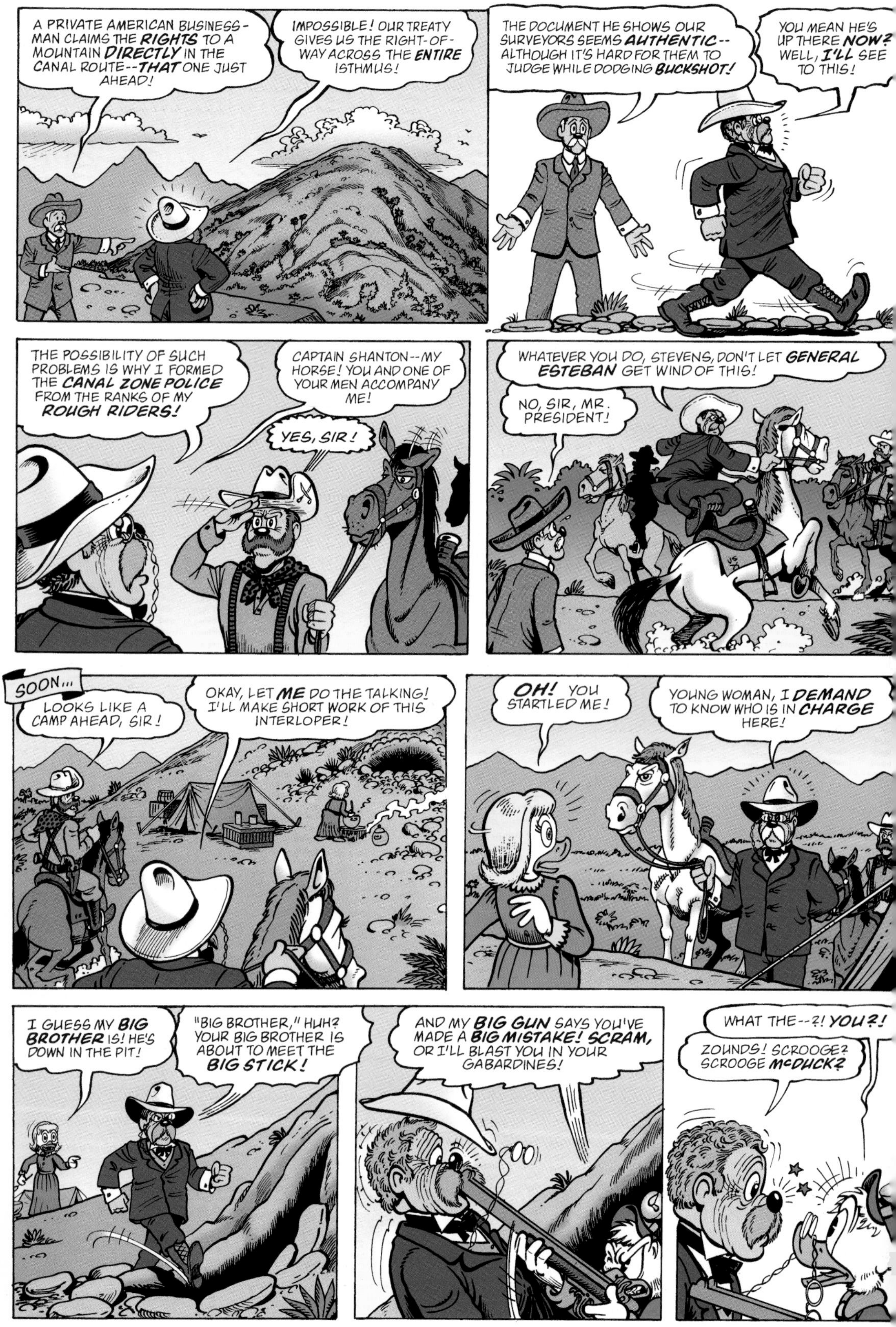
A PRIVATE AMERICAN BUSINESS-MAN CLAIMS THE RIGHTS TO A MOUNTAIN DIRECTLY IN THE CANAL ROUTE--THAT ONE JUST AHEAD!
IMPOSSIBLE! OUR TREATY GIVES US THE RIGHT-OF-WAY ACROSS THE ENTIRE ISTHMUS!
THE DOCUMENT HE SHOWS OUR SURVEYORS SEEMS AUTHENTIC-- ALTHOUGH IT'S HARD FOR THEM TO JUDGE WHILE DODGING BUCKSHOT!
YOU MEAN HE'S UP THERE NOW? WELL, I'LL SEE TO THIS!
THE POSSIBILITY OF SUCH PROBLEMS IS WHY I FORMED THE CANAL ZONE POLICE FROM THE RANKS OF MY ROUGH RIDERS!
CAPTAIN SHANTON--MY HORSE! YOU AND ONE OF YOUR MEN ACCOMPANY ME!
YES, SIR!
WHATEVER YOU DO, STEVENS, DON'T LET GENERAL ESTEBAN GET WIND OF THIS!
NO, SIR, MR. PRESIDENT!
SOON...
LOOKS LIKE A CAMP AHEAD, SIR!
OKAY, LET ME DO THE TALKING! I'LL MAKE SHORT WORK OF THIS INTERLOPER!
OH! YOU STARTLED ME!
YOUNG WOMAN, I DEMAND TO KNOW WHO IS IN CHARGE HERE!
I GUESS MY BIG BROTHER IS! HE'S DOWN IN THE PIT!
"BIG BROTHER," HUH? YOUR BIG BROTHER IS ABOUT TO MEET THE BIG STICK!
AND MY BIG GUN SAYS YOU'VE MADE A BIG MISTAKE! SCRAM, OR I'LL BLAST YOU IN YOUR GABARDINES!
WHAT THE--?! YOU?!
ZOUNDS! SCROOGE? SCROOGE McDUCK?

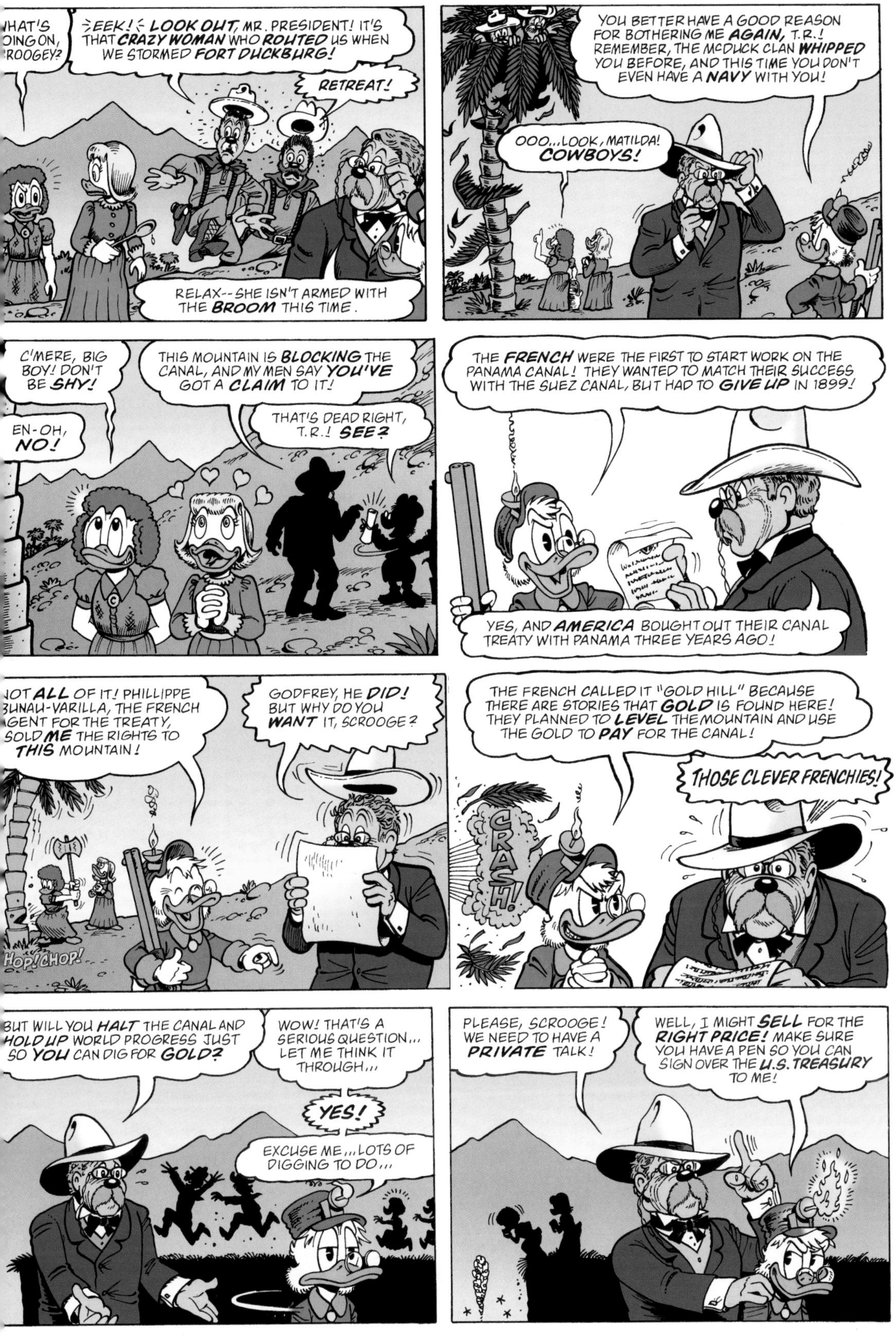
HAT'S
OING ON,
ROOGEY?
EEK! LOOK OUT, MR. PRESIDENT! IT'S THAT CRAZY WOMAN WHO ROUTED US WHEN WE STORMED FORT DUCKBURG!
RETREAT!
RELAX-- SHE ISN'T ARMED WITH THE BROOM THIS TIME.
YOU BETTER HAVE A GOOD REASON FOR BOTHERING ME AGAIN, T.R.! REMEMBER, THE McDUCK CLAN WHIPPED YOU BEFORE, AND THIS TIME YOU DON'T EVEN HAVE A NAVY WITH YOU!
OOO... LOOK, MATILDA! COWBOYS!
C'MERE, BIG BOY! DON'T BE SHY!
EN-OH, NO!
THIS MOUNTAIN IS BLOCKING THE CANAL, AND MY MEN SAY YOU'VE GOT A CLAIM TO IT!
THAT'S DEAD RIGHT, T.R.! SEE?
THE FRENCH WERE THE FIRST TO START WORK ON THE PANAMA CANAL! THEY WANTED TO MATCH THEIR SUCCESS WITH THE SUEZ CANAL, BUT HAD TO GIVE UP IN 1899!
YES, AND AMERICA BOUGHT OUT THEIR CANAL TREATY WITH PANAMA THREE YEARS AGO!
NOT ALL OF IT! PHILLIPPE BUNAU-VARILLA, THE FRENCH AGENT FOR THE TREATY, SOLD ME THE RIGHTS TO THIS MOUNTAIN!
GODFREY, HE DID! BUT WHY DO YOU WANT IT, SCROOGE?
HOP! CHOP!
THE FRENCH CALLED IT "GOLD HILL" BECAUSE THERE ARE STORIES THAT GOLD IS FOUND HERE! THEY PLANNED TO LEVEL THE MOUNTAIN AND USE THE GOLD TO PAY FOR THE CANAL!
THOSE CLEVER FRENCHIES!
CRASH!
BUT WILL YOU HALT THE CANAL AND HOLD UP WORLD PROGRESS JUST SO YOU CAN DIG FOR GOLD?
WOW! THAT'S A SERIOUS QUESTION... LET ME THINK IT THROUGH...
YES!
EXCUSE ME... LOTS OF DIGGING TO DO...
PLEASE, SCROOGE! WE NEED TO HAVE A PRIVATE TALK!
WELL, I MIGHT SELL FOR THE RIGHT PRICE! MAKE SURE YOU HAVE A PEN SO YOU CAN SIGN OVER THE U.S. TREASURY TO ME!

SOON, IN **RAILCAR ONE**, ON THE PRESIDENTIAL TRAIN...

YOOHOO! COWBOY! HEY, CUTEY! COME OVER HERE!

HORTENSE, **PLEASE** STOP FLIRTING WITH THE ROUGH RIDERS!

WE'RE TRYING TO HOLD A SECRET PRESIDENTIAL SUMMIT MEETING HERE, YOUNG LADY!

AW, GO SOAK YOUR HEAD! **BOTH** OF YOU!

AND **YOU**, TEDDY--DON'T EVEN **SPEAK** TO ME UNTIL YOU GRANT WOMEN THE RIGHT TO VOTE, YOU @*#%!!!

SUCH A **TEMPER**!

≥SIGH!≤

WOW! CUSSING OUT THE PRESIDENT OF THE UNITED STATES!

THAT'S MY MA!

≥SIGH!≤

SCROOGE, THERE'S A **PANAMANIAN GENERAL** WHO'LL LAUNCH A MILITARY **COUP D'ETAT** IF HE LEARNS OF ANY HANKY-PANKY IN THE CANAL TREATY!

I'M NOT CONCERNED WITH YOUR **POLITICAL** PROBLEMS! YOU CAN HAVE THE RIGHTS TO MY "GOLD HILL" WHEN I'M **DONE DIGGING**!

WITH A **SHOVEL**? THAT WILL TAKE **YEARS**!

LOOK, IF I HELP YOU GET THE JOB DONE **FASTER**, WILL THAT SATISFY YOU?

AT **YOUR** EXPENSE? **SURE**!

I'D HAVE TO DEAL WITH IT **PERSONALLY** SO NOT A SOUL WILL LEARN OF IT... HM...

IT WILL BE AN **ADVENTURE**! JUST LIKE OUR DAYS BACK IN THE DAKOTA BADLANDS!

IT'S A **DEAL**! LET'S **DRINK** TO IT!

TO THE SECRET ROOSEVELT-McDUCK TREATY!

CLINK!

YES, THE **McDUCK-ROOSEVELT TREATY**!

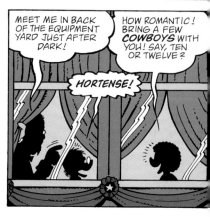

MEET ME IN BACK OF THE EQUIPMENT YARD JUST AFTER DARK!

HOW ROMANTIC! BRING A FEW **COWBOYS** WITH YOU! SAY, TEN OR TWELVE?

HORTENSE!

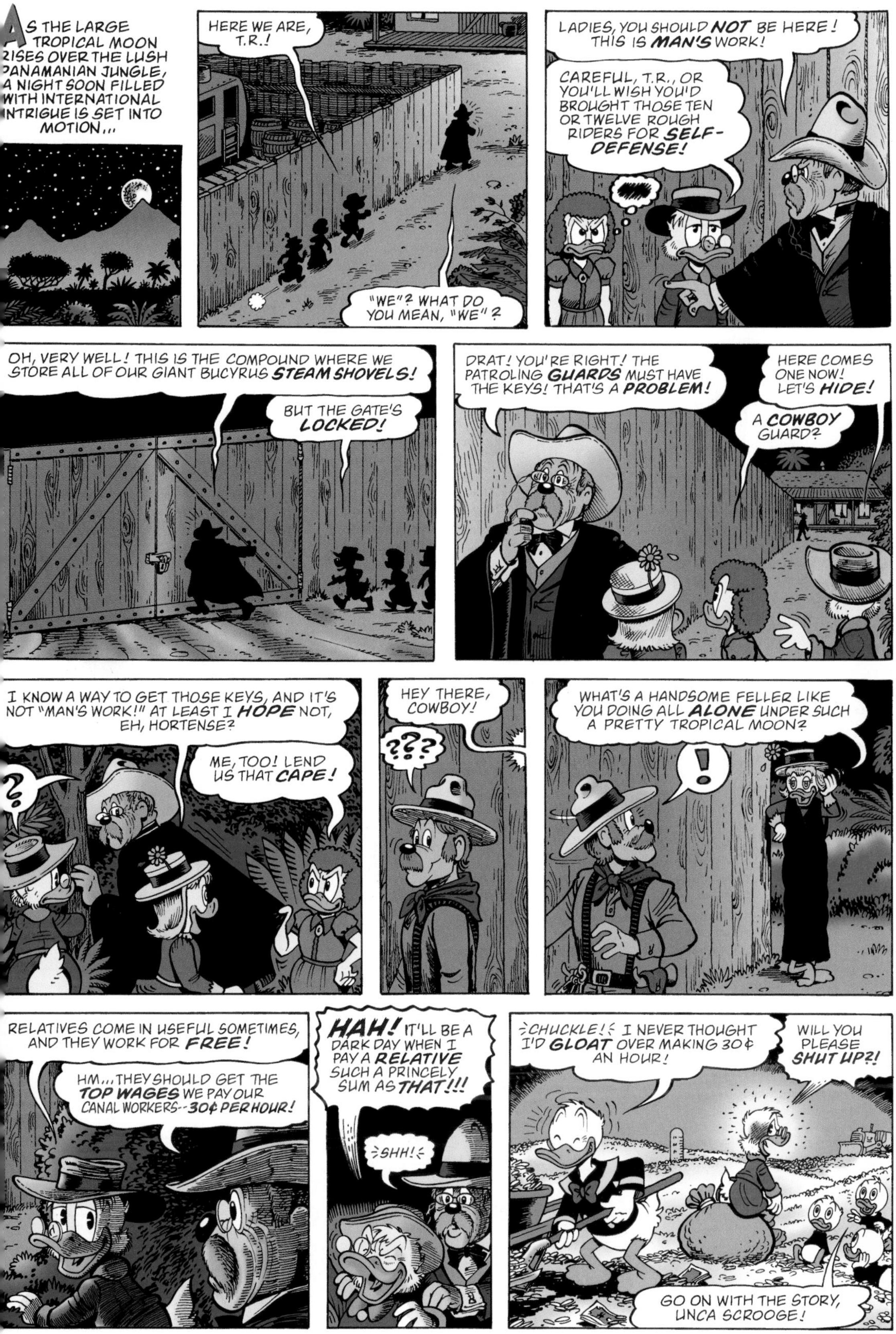
AS THE LARGE TROPICAL MOON RISES OVER THE LUSH PANAMANIAN JUNGLE, A NIGHT SOON FILLED WITH INTERNATIONAL INTRIGUE IS SET INTO MOTION...
HERE WE ARE, T.R.!
"WE"? WHAT DO YOU MEAN, "WE"?
LADIES, YOU SHOULD NOT BE HERE! THIS IS MAN'S WORK!
CAREFUL, T.R., OR YOU'LL WISH YOU'D BROUGHT THOSE TEN OR TWELVE ROUGH RIDERS FOR SELF-DEFENSE!
OH, VERY WELL! THIS IS THE COMPOUND WHERE WE STORE ALL OF OUR GIANT BUCYRUS STEAM SHOVELS!
BUT THE GATE'S LOCKED!
DRAT! YOU'RE RIGHT! THE PATROLING GUARDS MUST HAVE THE KEYS! THAT'S A PROBLEM!
HERE COMES ONE NOW! LET'S HIDE!
A COWBOY GUARD?
I KNOW A WAY TO GET THOSE KEYS, AND IT'S NOT "MAN'S WORK!" AT LEAST I HOPE NOT, EH, HORTENSE?
?
ME, TOO! LEND US THAT CAPE!
HEY THERE, COWBOY!
???
WHAT'S A HANDSOME FELLER LIKE YOU DOING ALL ALONE UNDER SUCH A PRETTY TROPICAL MOON?
!
RELATIVES COME IN USEFUL SOMETIMES, AND THEY WORK FOR FREE!
HM...THEY SHOULD GET THE TOP WAGES WE PAY OUR CANAL WORKERS--30¢ PER HOUR!
HAH! IT'LL BE A DARK DAY WHEN I PAY A RELATIVE SUCH A PRINCELY SUM AS THAT!!!
SHH!
CHUCKLE! I NEVER THOUGHT I'D GLOAT OVER MAKING 30¢ AN HOUR!
WILL YOU PLEASE SHUT UP?!
GO ON WITH THE STORY, UNCA SCROOGE!

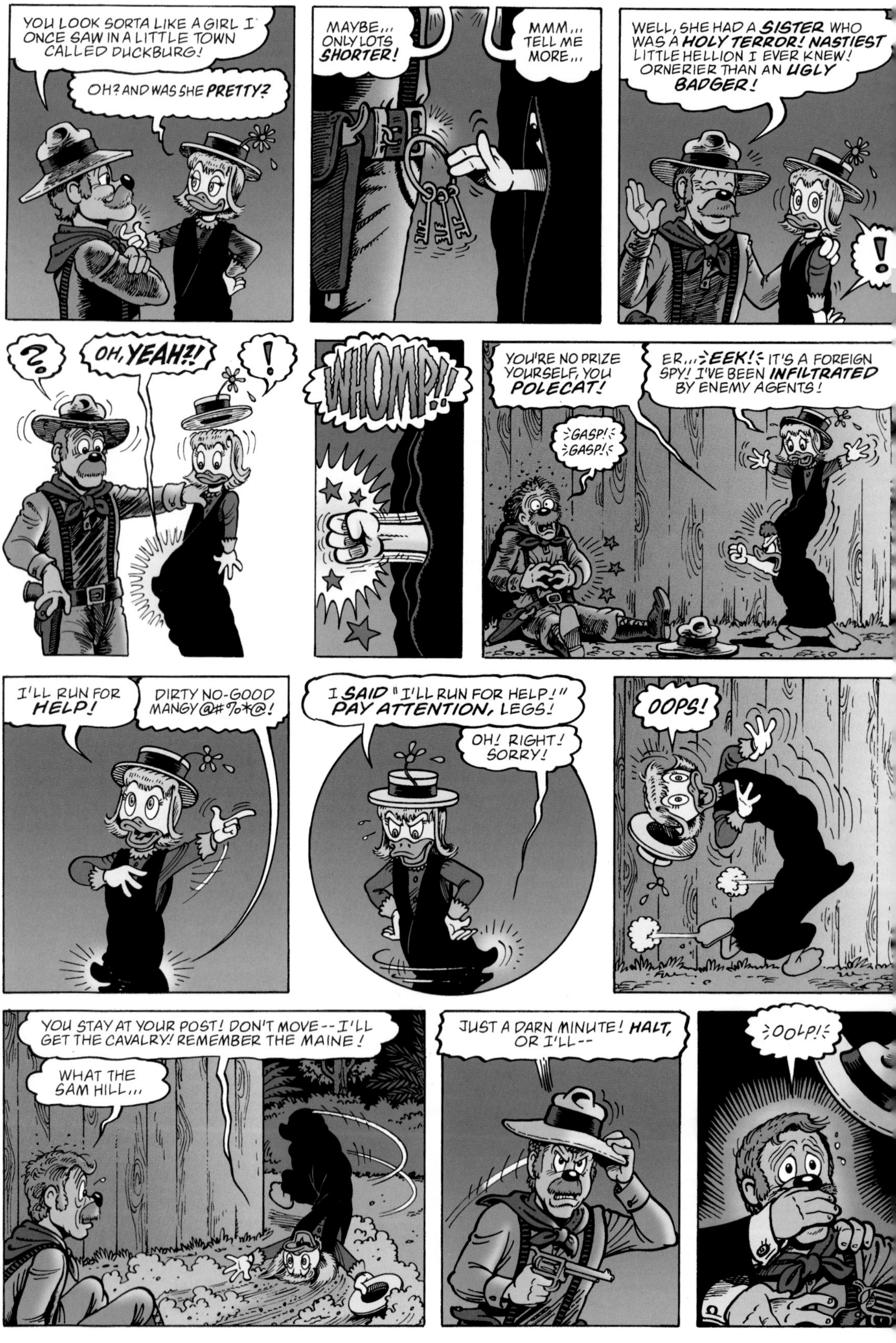

YOU LOOK SORTA LIKE A GIRL I ONCE SAW IN A LITTLE TOWN CALLED DUCKBURG!
OH? AND WAS SHE PRETTY?
MAYBE... ONLY LOTS SHORTER!
MMM... TELL ME MORE...
WELL, SHE HAD A SISTER WHO WAS A HOLY TERROR! NASTIEST LITTLE HELLION I EVER KNEW! ORNERIER THAN AN UGLY BADGER!
!
?
OH, YEAH?!
!
WHOMP!!
YOU'RE NO PRIZE YOURSELF, YOU POLECAT!
ER... EEK! IT'S A FOREIGN SPY! I'VE BEEN INFILTRATED BY ENEMY AGENTS!
GASP! GASP!
I'LL RUN FOR HELP!
DIRTY NO-GOOD MANGY @#%*@!
I SAID "I'LL RUN FOR HELP!" PAY ATTENTION, LEGS!
OH! RIGHT! SORRY!
OOPS!
YOU STAY AT YOUR POST! DON'T MOVE -- I'LL GET THE CAVALRY! REMEMBER THE MAINE!
WHAT THE SAM HILL...
JUST A DARN MINUTE! HALT, OR I'LL --
OOLP!

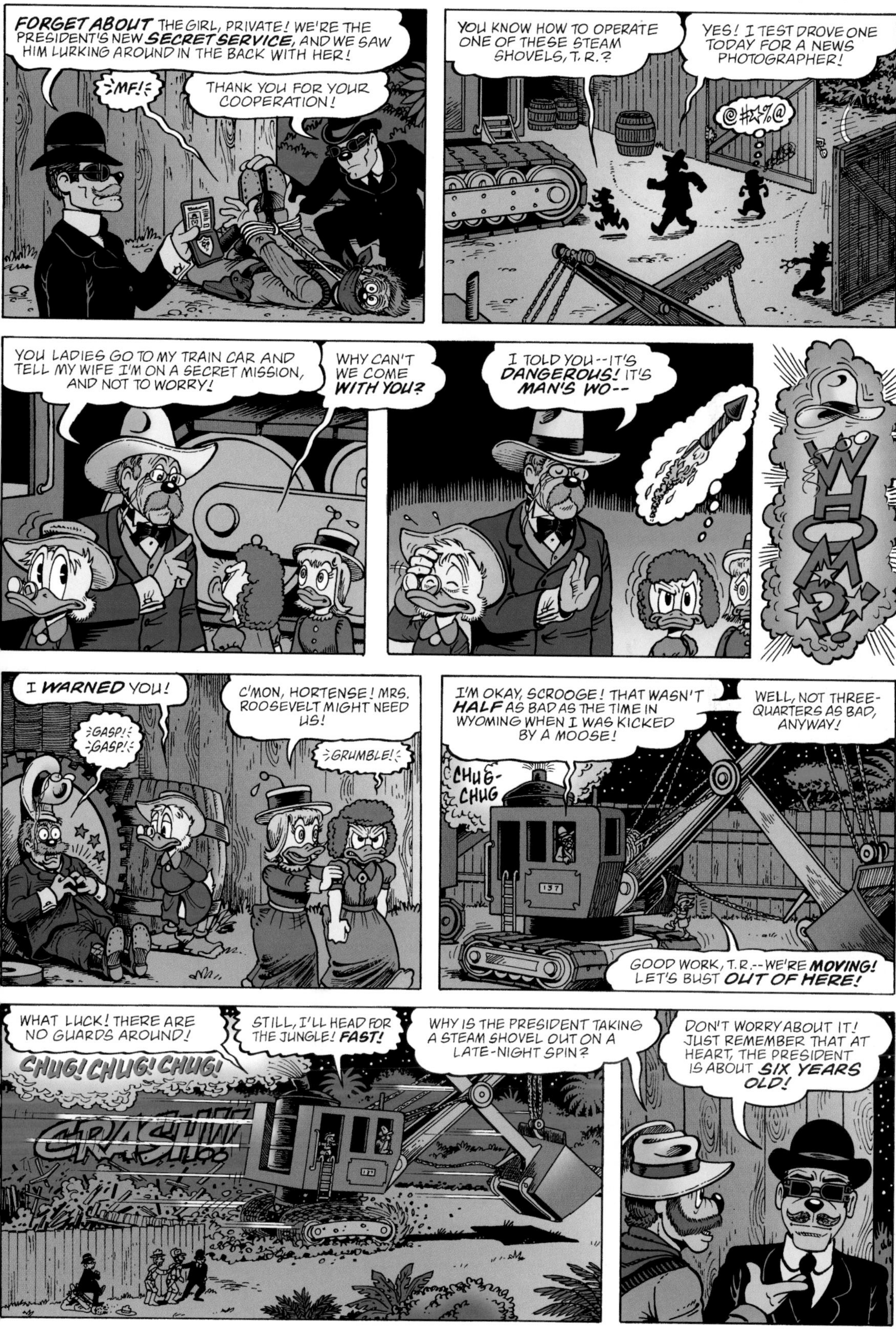
FORGET ABOUT THE GIRL, PRIVATE! WE'RE THE PRESIDENT'S NEW SECRET SERVICE, AND WE SAW HIM LURKING AROUND IN THE BACK WITH HER!
MF!
THANK YOU FOR YOUR COOPERATION!
YOU KNOW HOW TO OPERATE ONE OF THESE STEAM SHOVELS, T.R.?
YES! I TEST DROVE ONE TODAY FOR A NEWS PHOTOGRAPHER!
@#☆%@
YOU LADIES GO TO MY TRAIN CAR AND TELL MY WIFE I'M ON A SECRET MISSION, AND NOT TO WORRY!
WHY CAN'T WE COME WITH YOU?
I TOLD YOU--IT'S DANGEROUS! IT'S MAN'S WO--
WHAM!
I WARNED YOU!
GASP! GASP!
C'MON, HORTENSE! MRS. ROOSEVELT MIGHT NEED US!
GRUMBLE!
I'M OKAY, SCROOGE! THAT WASN'T HALF AS BAD AS THE TIME IN WYOMING WHEN I WAS KICKED BY A MOOSE!
WELL, NOT THREE-QUARTERS AS BAD, ANYWAY!
CHUG-CHUG
137
GOOD WORK, T.R.--WE'RE MOVING! LET'S BUST OUT OF HERE!
WHAT LUCK! THERE ARE NO GUARDS AROUND!
STILL, I'LL HEAD FOR THE JUNGLE! FAST!
CHUG! CHUG! CHUG!
CRASH!
WHY IS THE PRESIDENT TAKING A STEAM SHOVEL OUT ON A LATE-NIGHT SPIN?
DON'T WORRY ABOUT IT! JUST REMEMBER THAT AT HEART, THE PRESIDENT IS ABOUT SIX YEARS OLD!

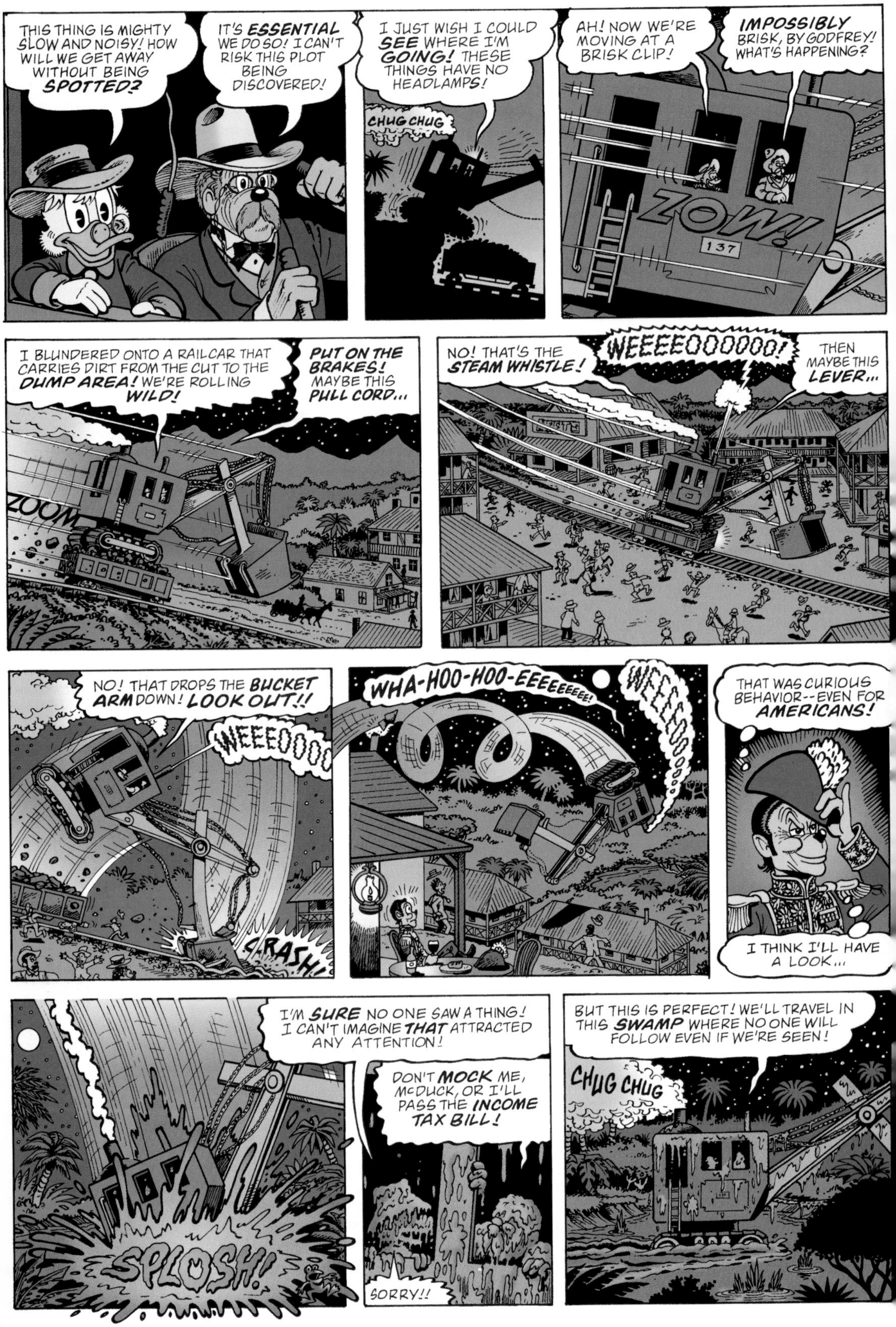
THIS THING IS MIGHTY SLOW AND NOISY! HOW WILL WE GET AWAY WITHOUT BEING SPOTTED?
IT'S ESSENTIAL WE DO SO! I CAN'T RISK THIS PLOT BEING DISCOVERED!
I JUST WISH I COULD SEE WHERE I'M GOING! THESE THINGS HAVE NO HEADLAMPS!
CHUG CHUG
AH! NOW WE'RE MOVING AT A BRISK CLIP!
IMPOSSIBLY BRISK, BY GODFREY! WHAT'S HAPPENING?
ZOW!
137
I BLUNDERED ONTO A RAILCAR THAT CARRIES DIRT FROM THE CUT TO THE DUMP AREA! WE'RE ROLLING WILD!
PUT ON THE BRAKES! MAYBE THIS PULL CORD...
ZOOM
NO! THAT'S THE STEAM WHISTLE!
WEEEEOOOOOOO!
THEN MAYBE THIS LEVER...
NO! THAT DROPS THE BUCKET ARM DOWN! LOOK OUT!!
WEEEOOOO
CRASH!
WHA-HOO-HOO-EEEEeeeee!
WEEEOOOooo
THAT WAS CURIOUS BEHAVIOR--EVEN FOR AMERICANS!
I THINK I'LL HAVE A LOOK...
SPLOSH!
I'M SURE NO ONE SAW A THING! I CAN'T IMAGINE THAT ATTRACTED ANY ATTENTION!
DON'T MOCK ME, McDUCK, OR I'LL PASS THE INCOME TAX BILL!
SORRY!!
BUT THIS IS PERFECT! WE'LL TRAVEL IN THIS SWAMP WHERE NO ONE WILL FOLLOW EVEN IF WE'RE SEEN!
CHUG CHUG

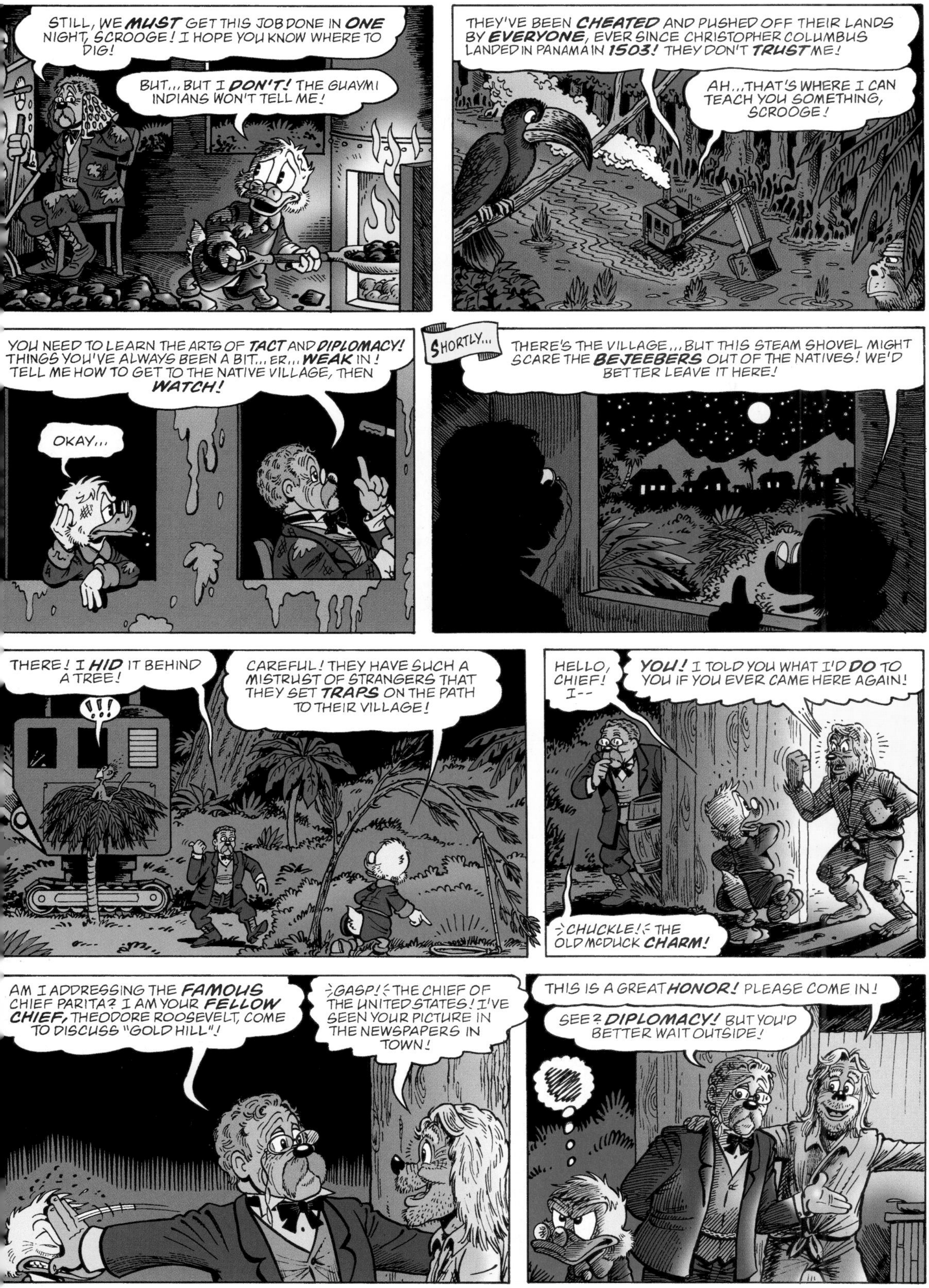
STILL, WE MUST GET THIS JOB DONE IN ONE NIGHT, SCROOGE! I HOPE YOU KNOW WHERE TO DIG!
BUT... BUT I DON'T! THE GUAYMI INDIANS WON'T TELL ME!
THEY'VE BEEN CHEATED AND PUSHED OFF THEIR LANDS BY EVERYONE, EVER SINCE CHRISTOPHER COLUMBUS LANDED IN PANAMA IN 1503! THEY DON'T TRUST ME!
AH... THAT'S WHERE I CAN TEACH YOU SOMETHING, SCROOGE!
YOU NEED TO LEARN THE ARTS OF TACT AND DIPLOMACY! THINGS YOU'VE ALWAYS BEEN A BIT... ER... WEAK IN! TELL ME HOW TO GET TO THE NATIVE VILLAGE, THEN WATCH!
OKAY...
SHORTLY...
THERE'S THE VILLAGE... BUT THIS STEAM SHOVEL MIGHT SCARE THE BEJEEBERS OUT OF THE NATIVES! WE'D BETTER LEAVE IT HERE!
THERE! I HID IT BEHIND A TREE!
!!!
CAREFUL! THEY HAVE SUCH A MISTRUST OF STRANGERS THAT THEY SET TRAPS ON THE PATH TO THEIR VILLAGE!
HELLO, CHIEF! I--
YOU! I TOLD YOU WHAT I'D DO TO YOU IF YOU EVER CAME HERE AGAIN!
CHUCKLE! THE OLD McDUCK CHARM!
AM I ADDRESSING THE FAMOUS CHIEF PARITA? I AM YOUR FELLOW CHIEF, THEODORE ROOSEVELT, COME TO DISCUSS "GOLD HILL"!
GASP! THE CHIEF OF THE UNITED STATES! I'VE SEEN YOUR PICTURE IN THE NEWSPAPERS IN TOWN!
THIS IS A GREAT HONOR! PLEASE COME IN!
SEE? DIPLOMACY! BUT YOU'D BETTER WAIT OUTSIDE!

SIT, **SIT**, MY FRIEND! HAVE SOME OF OUR TRIBAL DRINK, **CHICHA**! I WILL GET A MAP OF "GOLD HILL"!

BULLY! DEE-LIGHTED!

≶PST!≶ T.R.! IS EVERYTHING OKAY?

QUITE, SCROOGE! THE CHIEF IS GETTING HIS MAP!

I CAN'T UNDERSTAND IT! THE GUAYMI ARE NOT USUALLY SO **OPEN** TO A STRANGER WITHOUT FIRST **TESTING** HIS WORTHINESS!

AND HOW DO THEY CONDUCT THIS QUAINT TEST?

WITH A SLEEP TONIC MADE FROM MASTICATED CORN! THEY CALL IT **CHICHA**!

WHATEVER YOU DO, T.R., **STAY AWAY** FROM THAT STUFF! IT'S **MURDER**!

T.R.?

T.R.?

OH, **NO**! HE'S **OUT** LIKE A LIGHT! AND THE CHIEF IS READY TO TALK **NOW**! WHAT TO DO, WHAT TO DO...

HEY! THAT CHICHA WAS SWELL! REALLY... ER...**BULLY**!

I AM PLEASED YOU LIKE IT! YOU HAVE **PROVEN** YOURSELF A STRONG AND BRAVE FRIEND!

MY POOR FRIEND! YOUR **ARM** IS SO THIN AND **PALE**!

ER...YES, I HAVE A TOUCH OF YOUR PANAMANIAN **MALARIA**! BUT HURRY-- LET'S SEE THAT **MAP**!

I'LL SHOW YOU WHERE GOLD HAS BEEN FOUND FOR CENTURIES, BUT **FIRST**, SHOW ME WHERE THAT **AWFUL** McDUCK IS ALREADY DIGGING!

BUT I CAN'T SEE THE-- ER...I MEAN, **SURE**!

RIGHT **THERE**!

POK!

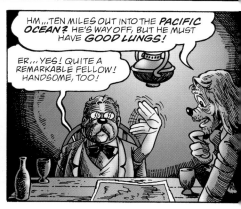

HM...TEN MILES OUT INTO THE **PACIFIC OCEAN**? HE'S WAY OFF, BUT HE MUST HAVE **GOOD LUNGS**!

ER...YES! QUITE A REMARKABLE FELLOW! HANDSOME, TOO!

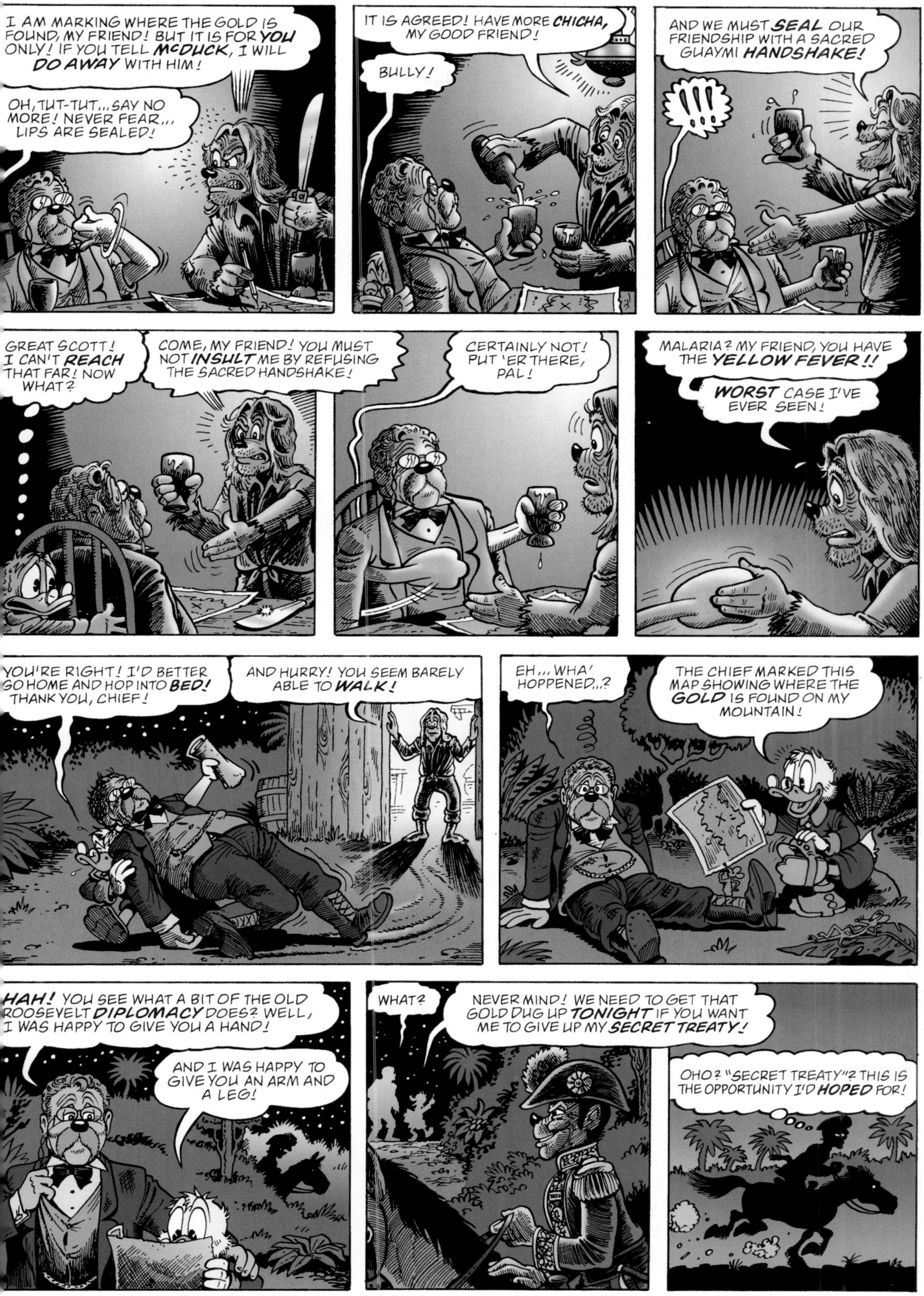
I AM MARKING WHERE THE GOLD IS FOUND, MY FRIEND! BUT IT IS FOR YOU ONLY! IF YOU TELL McDUCK, I WILL DO AWAY WITH HIM!
OH, TUT-TUT... SAY NO MORE! NEVER FEAR... LIPS ARE SEALED!
IT IS AGREED! HAVE MORE CHICHA, MY GOOD FRIEND!
BULLY!
AND WE MUST SEAL OUR FRIENDSHIP WITH A SACRED GUAYMI HANDSHAKE!
!!!
GREAT SCOTT! I CAN'T REACH THAT FAR! NOW WHAT?
COME, MY FRIEND! YOU MUST NOT INSULT ME BY REFUSING THE SACRED HANDSHAKE!
CERTAINLY NOT! PUT 'ER THERE, PAL!
MALARIA? MY FRIEND, YOU HAVE THE YELLOW FEVER!!
WORST CASE I'VE EVER SEEN!
YOU'RE RIGHT! I'D BETTER GO HOME AND HOP INTO BED! THANK YOU, CHIEF!
AND HURRY! YOU SEEM BARELY ABLE TO WALK!
EH... WHA' HOPPENED...?
THE CHIEF MARKED THIS MAP SHOWING WHERE THE GOLD IS FOUND ON MY MOUNTAIN!
HAH! YOU SEE WHAT A BIT OF THE OLD ROOSEVELT DIPLOMACY DOES? WELL, I WAS HAPPY TO GIVE YOU A HAND!
AND I WAS HAPPY TO GIVE YOU AN ARM AND A LEG!
WHAT?
NEVER MIND! WE NEED TO GET THAT GOLD DUG UP TONIGHT IF YOU WANT ME TO GIVE UP MY SECRET TREATY!
OHO? "SECRET TREATY"? THIS IS THE OPPORTUNITY I'D HOPED FOR!

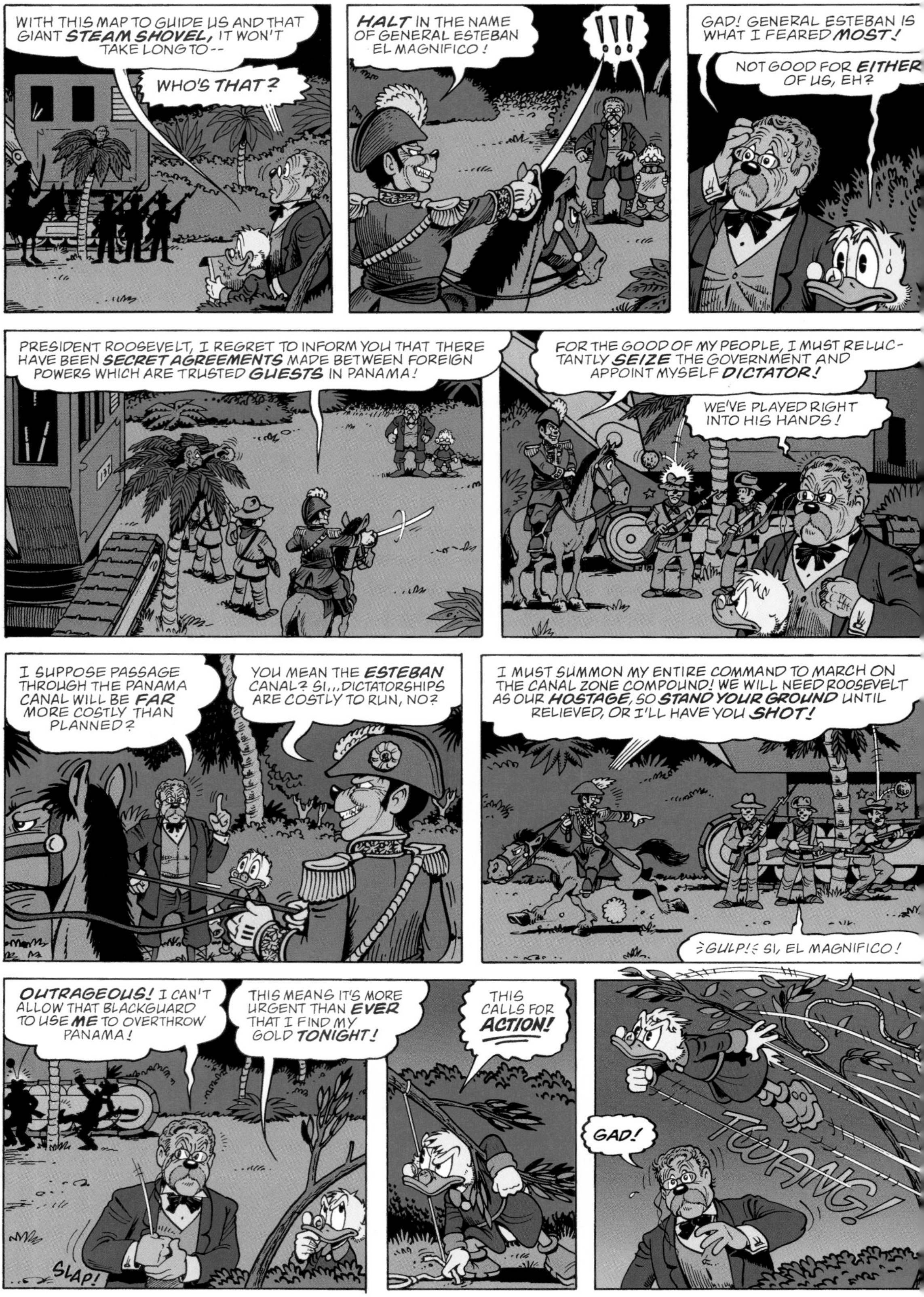

WITH THIS MAP TO GUIDE US AND THAT GIANT STEAM SHOVEL, IT WON'T TAKE LONG TO --
WHO'S THAT?
HALT IN THE NAME OF GENERAL ESTEBAN EL MAGNIFICO!
!!!
GAD! GENERAL ESTEBAN IS WHAT I FEARED MOST!
NOT GOOD FOR EITHER OF US, EH?
PRESIDENT ROOSEVELT, I REGRET TO INFORM YOU THAT THERE HAVE BEEN SECRET AGREEMENTS MADE BETWEEN FOREIGN POWERS WHICH ARE TRUSTED GUESTS IN PANAMA!
FOR THE GOOD OF MY PEOPLE, I MUST RELUCTANTLY SEIZE THE GOVERNMENT AND APPOINT MYSELF DICTATOR!
WE'VE PLAYED RIGHT INTO HIS HANDS!
I SUPPOSE PASSAGE THROUGH THE PANAMA CANAL WILL BE FAR MORE COSTLY THAN PLANNED?
YOU MEAN THE ESTEBAN CANAL? SI... DICTATORSHIPS ARE COSTLY TO RUN, NO?
I MUST SUMMON MY ENTIRE COMMAND TO MARCH ON THE CANAL ZONE COMPOUND! WE WILL NEED ROOSEVELT AS OUR HOSTAGE, SO STAND YOUR GROUND UNTIL RELIEVED, OR I'LL HAVE YOU SHOT!
GULP! SI, EL MAGNIFICO!
OUTRAGEOUS! I CAN'T ALLOW THAT BLACKGUARD TO USE ME TO OVERTHROW PANAMA!
THIS MEANS IT'S MORE URGENT THAN EVER THAT I FIND MY GOLD TONIGHT!
SLAP!
THIS CALLS FOR ACTION!
GAD!
TWANG!

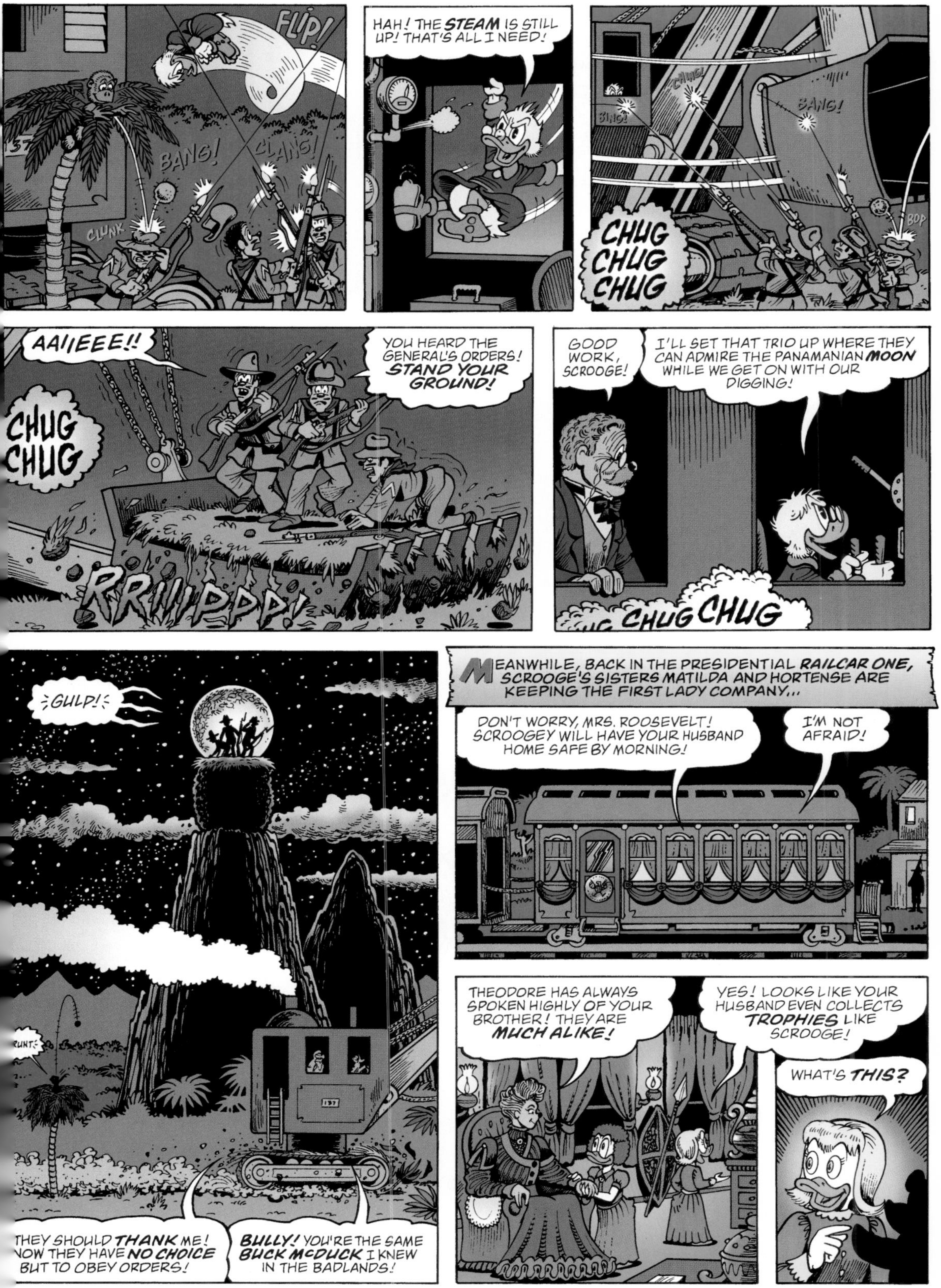

FLIP!
BANG!
CLANG!
CLUNK
HAH! THE STEAM IS STILL UP! THAT'S ALL I NEED!
BANG!
BOP
CHUG CHUG CHUG
AAIIEEE!!
YOU HEARD THE GENERAL'S ORDERS! STAND YOUR GROUND!
CHUG CHUG
RRIIIPPP!
GOOD WORK, SCROOGE!
I'LL SET THAT TRIO UP WHERE THEY CAN ADMIRE THE PANAMANIAN MOON WHILE WE GET ON WITH OUR DIGGING!
CHUG CHUG
GULP!
THEY SHOULD THANK ME! NOW THEY HAVE NO CHOICE BUT TO OBEY ORDERS!
BULLY! YOU'RE THE SAME BUCK McDUCK I KNEW IN THE BADLANDS!
MEANWHILE, BACK IN THE PRESIDENTIAL RAILCAR ONE, SCROOGE'S SISTERS MATILDA AND HORTENSE ARE KEEPING THE FIRST LADY COMPANY...
DON'T WORRY, MRS. ROOSEVELT! SCROOGEY WILL HAVE YOUR HUSBAND HOME SAFE BY MORNING!
I'M NOT AFRAID!
THEODORE HAS ALWAYS SPOKEN HIGHLY OF YOUR BROTHER! THEY ARE MUCH ALIKE!
YES! LOOKS LIKE YOUR HUSBAND EVEN COLLECTS TROPHIES LIKE SCROOGE!
WHAT'S THIS?

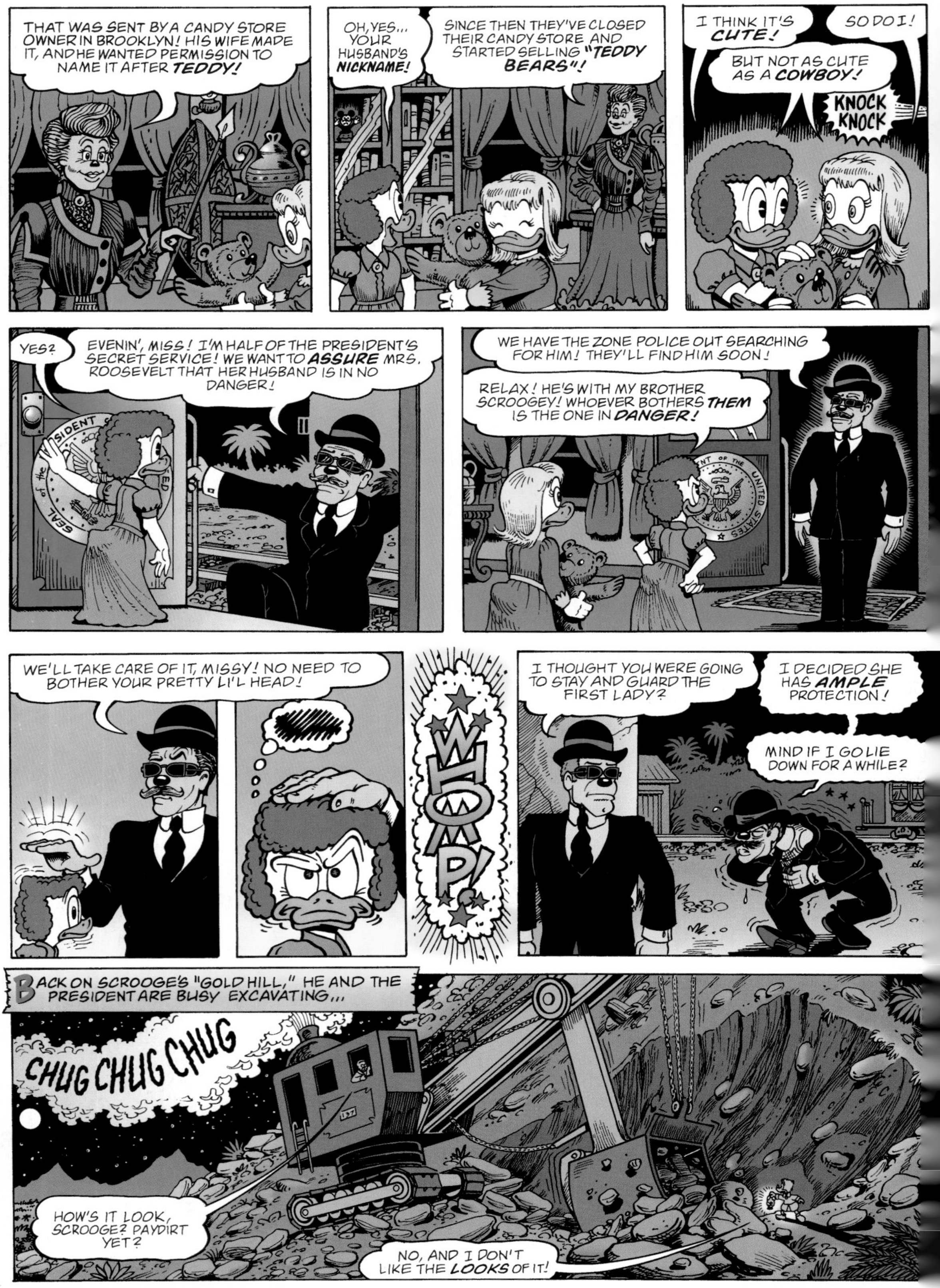
THAT WAS SENT BY A CANDY STORE OWNER IN BROOKLYN! HIS WIFE MADE IT, AND HE WANTED PERMISSION TO NAME IT AFTER TEDDY!
OH, YES... YOUR HUSBAND'S NICKNAME!
SINCE THEN THEY'VE CLOSED THEIR CANDY STORE AND STARTED SELLING "TEDDY BEARS"!
I THINK IT'S CUTE!
SO DO I!
BUT NOT AS CUTE AS A COWBOY!
KNOCK KNOCK
YES?
EVENIN', MISS! I'M HALF OF THE PRESIDENT'S SECRET SERVICE! WE WANT TO ASSURE MRS. ROOSEVELT THAT HER HUSBAND IS IN NO DANGER!
WE HAVE THE ZONE POLICE OUT SEARCHING FOR HIM! THEY'LL FIND HIM SOON!
RELAX! HE'S WITH MY BROTHER SCROOGEY! WHOEVER BOTHERS THEM IS THE ONE IN DANGER!
WE'LL TAKE CARE OF IT, MISSY! NO NEED TO BOTHER YOUR PRETTY LI'L HEAD!
WHOMP!
I THOUGHT YOU WERE GOING TO STAY AND GUARD THE FIRST LADY?
I DECIDED SHE HAS AMPLE PROTECTION!
MIND IF I GO LIE DOWN FOR A WHILE?
BACK ON SCROOGE'S "GOLD HILL," HE AND THE PRESIDENT ARE BUSY EXCAVATING...
CHUG CHUG CHUG
HOW'S IT LOOK, SCROOGE? PAYDIRT YET?
NO, AND I DON'T LIKE THE LOOKS OF IT!

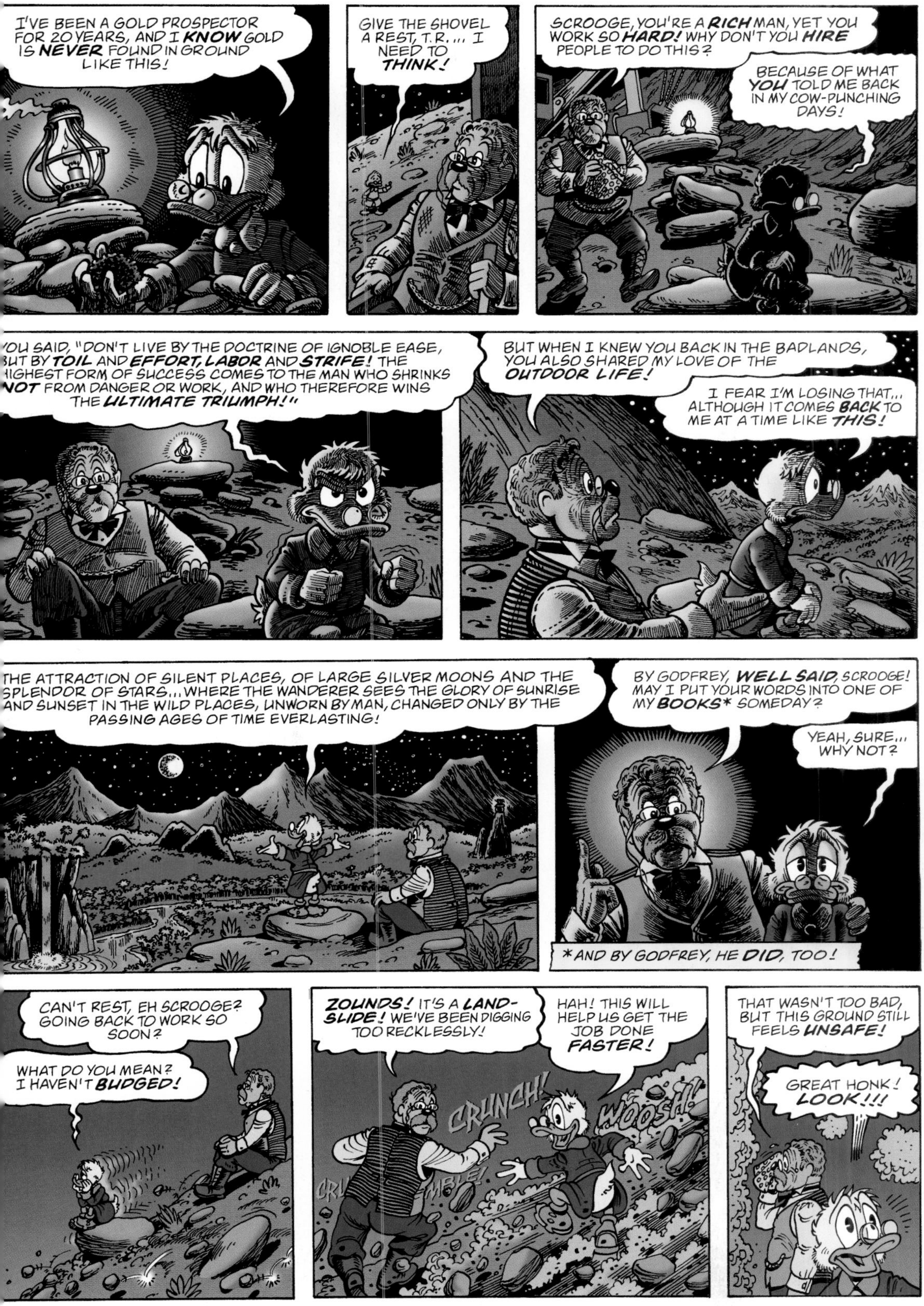
I'VE BEEN A GOLD PROSPECTOR FOR 20 YEARS, AND I KNOW GOLD IS NEVER FOUND IN GROUND LIKE THIS!
GIVE THE SHOVEL A REST, T.R.... I NEED TO THINK!
SCROOGE, YOU'RE A RICH MAN, YET YOU WORK SO HARD! WHY DON'T YOU HIRE PEOPLE TO DO THIS?
BECAUSE OF WHAT YOU TOLD ME BACK IN MY COW-PUNCHING DAYS!
YOU SAID, "DON'T LIVE BY THE DOCTRINE OF IGNOBLE EASE, BUT BY TOIL AND EFFORT, LABOR AND STRIFE! THE HIGHEST FORM OF SUCCESS COMES TO THE MAN WHO SHRINKS NOT FROM DANGER OR WORK, AND WHO THEREFORE WINS THE ULTIMATE TRIUMPH!"
BUT WHEN I KNEW YOU BACK IN THE BADLANDS, YOU ALSO SHARED MY LOVE OF THE OUTDOOR LIFE!
I FEAR I'M LOSING THAT... ALTHOUGH IT COMES BACK TO ME AT A TIME LIKE THIS!
THE ATTRACTION OF SILENT PLACES, OF LARGE SILVER MOONS AND THE SPLENDOR OF STARS... WHERE THE WANDERER SEES THE GLORY OF SUNRISE AND SUNSET IN THE WILD PLACES, UNWORN BY MAN, CHANGED ONLY BY THE PASSING AGES OF TIME EVERLASTING!
BY GODFREY, WELL SAID, SCROOGE! MAY I PUT YOUR WORDS INTO ONE OF MY BOOKS* SOMEDAY?
YEAH, SURE... WHY NOT?
*AND BY GODFREY, HE DID, TOO!
CAN'T REST, EH SCROOGE? GOING BACK TO WORK SO SOON?
WHAT DO YOU MEAN? I HAVEN'T BUDGED!
ZOUNDS! IT'S A LANDSLIDE! WE'VE BEEN DIGGING TOO RECKLESSLY!
HAH! THIS WILL HELP US GET THE JOB DONE FASTER!
CRUNCH!
WOOSH!
THAT WASN'T TOO BAD, BUT THIS GROUND STILL FEELS UNSAFE!
GREAT HONK! LOOK!!!

JEHOSOPHAT! A GIGANTIC STONE JAGUAR WITH **GOLDEN** FANGS AND CLAWS! THE GOLD THAT THE NATIVES FOUND HERE MUST HAVE BEEN **LEAFING** THAT PEELED OFF!

I'LL BE DOUBLE-JABBERED! THIS MUST HAVE BEEN **BURIED** HERE CENTURIES AGO TO **HIDE** IT FROM THE **SPANISH INVADERS!**

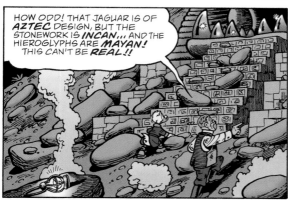

HOW ODD! THAT JAGUAR IS OF **AZTEC** DESIGN, BUT THE STONEWORK IS **INCAN**... AND THE HIEROGLYPHS ARE **MAYAN!** THIS CAN'T BE **REAL!!**

I KNOW! ALONG WITH OUR OTHER SHARED VALUES, I ALSO STUDY **HISTORY**, T.R.! WHAT'S MORE, I CAN **READ** ANCIENT MAYAN!

GOOD MAN, SCROOGE! WHAT DOES IT **SAY?**

THIS IS A TEMPLE OF OFFERINGS TO THE GODS FOR THE SUCCESS OF **COMMERCE**... OF TRADE BETWEEN **ALL** THE NATIONS OF PRE-COLUMBIAN AMERICA, NORTH AND SOUTH!

THIS ISTHMUS HAS ALWAYS BEEN A CHANNEL FOR INTERNATIONAL TRADE! NOW IT'S SOON TO BE **OCEAN** TO **OCEAN**, BUT IN ANCIENT TIMES IT WAS **CONTINENT** TO **CONTINENT!**

YUMMY! WHAT MIGHT BE **INSIDE?!**

MY STARS AND LITTLE COMETS! IT'S LIKE A *GIFTSTORE SHOW-ROOM* FOR TREASURE!

THESE MARKS REPRESENT INDIVIDUAL *YEARS* OF THE MAYAN CALENDAR, SO THE ITEMS ON EACH LEDGE MUST REPRESENT THE *GOD'S SHARE* OF THE GOODS THAT PASSED THROUGH ANCIENT PANAMA!

AZTEC FEATHER CLOAKS, *MAYAN* JADE, *INCAN* BLANKETS, *MIXTEC* SILVER CARVINGS, *OLMEC* SCULPTURES, *TOLTEC* STAR CHARTS, *ANASAZI* TURQUOISE, *MUISCAN* GOLD FROM ELDORADO!

SCROOGE, IT'S LIKE A FABULOUS *MUSEUM* OF ANCIENT AMERICAN CIVILIZATIONS!

AND *TREASURES!*

SCROOGE! *SURELY* YOU DON'T INTEND TO KEEP ALL THIS FOR *YOURSELF!*

OF *COURSE* I DO! I HAVE A *LEGAL CLAIM* TO THIS MOUNTAIN AND *EVERYTHING* ON IT!

BUT THESE ARE ALL *NATIONAL TREASURES* OF DOZENS OF CULTURES... FROM A *GLORIOUS* TIME WHEN THE PEOPLES OF TWO HEMISPHERES LIVED IN PEACE AND HARMONY!

BAH! THAT MEANS *NOTHING* TO ME!

SCROOGE McDUCK! AS PRESIDENT OF THE UNITED STATES, I *WON'T LET YOU DO IT!*

WHAT? WE HAVE A *DEAL!*

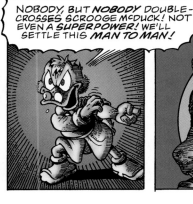

NOBODY, BUT *NOBODY* DOUBLE-CROSSES SCROOGE McDUCK! NOT EVEN A *SUPERPOWER!* WE'LL SETTLE THIS *MAN TO MAN!*

IF THAT'S YOUR CHOICE, VERY WELL! PUT UP YOUR DUKES!

COME AT ME, YA MONKEY!

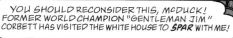
YOU SHOULD RECONSIDER THIS, McDUCK! FORMER WORLD CHAMPION "GENTLEMAN JIM" CORBETT HAS VISITED THE WHITE HOUSE TO **SPAR** WITH ME!

YEAH? DOES HE STILL HAVE THE SCAR OVER HIS EYE WHERE I **KAYOED** HIM IN 'FRISCO IN '91?

JAB!

CAREFUL, SCROOGE! THOSE ARE **PRICELESS ARTIFACTS!**

I DIDN'T TOUCH 'EM! BUT I WILL WHEN I **SELL** 'EM!

SOMETHING IS AMISS! I FEAR IT'S ANOTHER **LANDSLIDE!**

RUMBLE!

DON'T TRY TO **DISTRACT** ME WITH A MERE NATURAL DISASTER! YOU'RE GONNA GET A LICKING AND **LIKE** IT!

RUMBLE!

WHOOSH!

NEVER HEARD OF HIM!

I LEARNED INDIAN WRESTLING FROM **STANDING BULL** HIMSELF!

THEY STARTED CALLING HIM **SITTING BULL** AFTER OUR LAST MATCH!

SUITS ME! I CAN WHIP YOU AT **WRESTLING** AS EASILY AS **BOXING!**

IT'S TOO DIFFICULT TO STAND UP!

THEY NAMED THIS HOLD THE **"FULL McDUCK"** WHEN I DEMONSTRATED IT AT THE ST. LOUIS OLYMPICS TWO YEARS AGO!

>CHOKE!< I **YIELD!** >GASP!<

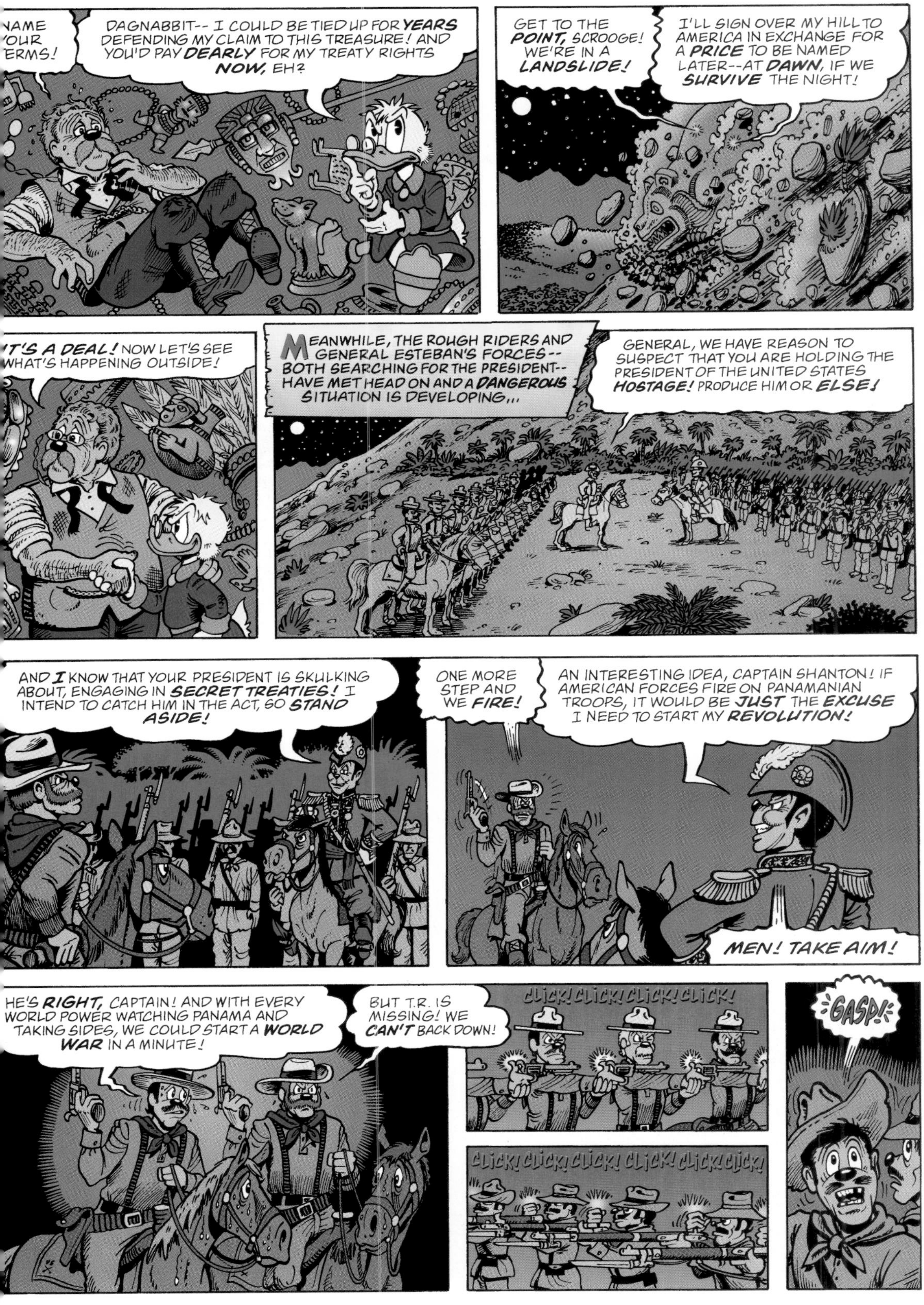
NAME YOUR TERMS!
DAGNABBIT-- I COULD BE TIED UP FOR YEARS DEFENDING MY CLAIM TO THIS TREASURE! AND YOU'D PAY DEARLY FOR MY TREATY RIGHTS NOW, EH?
GET TO THE POINT, SCROOGE! WE'RE IN A LANDSLIDE!
I'LL SIGN OVER MY HILL TO AMERICA IN EXCHANGE FOR A PRICE TO BE NAMED LATER--AT DAWN, IF WE SURVIVE THE NIGHT!
IT'S A DEAL! NOW LET'S SEE WHAT'S HAPPENING OUTSIDE!
MEANWHILE, THE ROUGH RIDERS AND GENERAL ESTEBAN'S FORCES -- BOTH SEARCHING FOR THE PRESIDENT-- HAVE MET HEAD ON AND A DANGEROUS SITUATION IS DEVELOPING...
GENERAL, WE HAVE REASON TO SUSPECT THAT YOU ARE HOLDING THE PRESIDENT OF THE UNITED STATES HOSTAGE! PRODUCE HIM OR ELSE!
AND I KNOW THAT YOUR PRESIDENT IS SKULKING ABOUT, ENGAGING IN SECRET TREATIES! I INTEND TO CATCH HIM IN THE ACT, SO STAND ASIDE!
ONE MORE STEP AND WE FIRE!
AN INTERESTING IDEA, CAPTAIN SHANTON! IF AMERICAN FORCES FIRE ON PANAMANIAN TROOPS, IT WOULD BE JUST THE EXCUSE I NEED TO START MY REVOLUTION!
MEN! TAKE AIM!
HE'S RIGHT, CAPTAIN! AND WITH EVERY WORLD POWER WATCHING PANAMA AND TAKING SIDES, WE COULD START A WORLD WAR IN A MINUTE!
BUT T.R. IS MISSING! WE CAN'T BACK DOWN!
CLICK! CLICK! CLICK! CLICK!
CLICK! CLICK! CLICK! CLICK! CLICK! CLICK!
GASP!

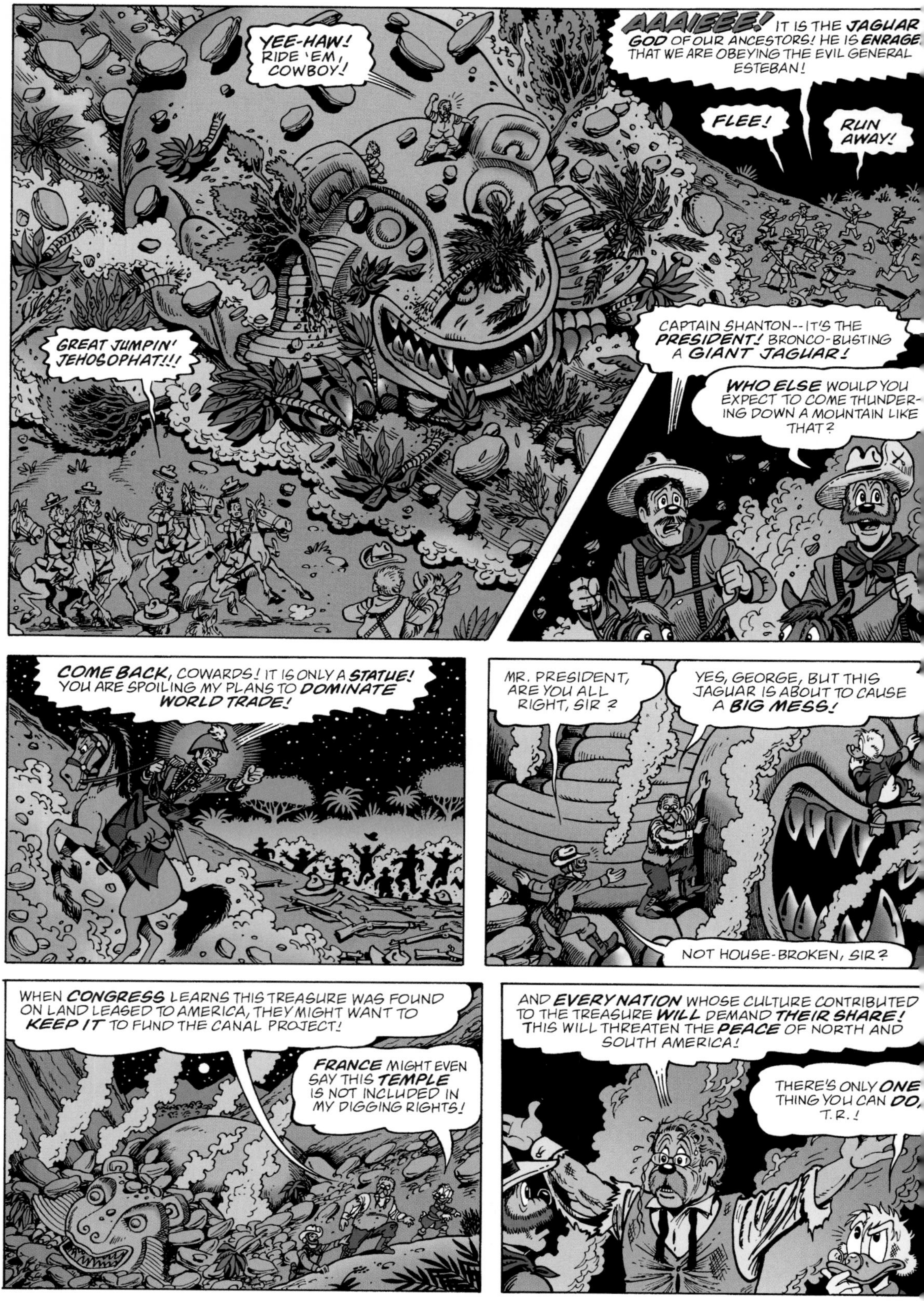
YEE-HAW! RIDE 'EM, COWBOY!
AAAIEEE! IT IS THE JAGUAR GOD OF OUR ANCESTORS! HE IS ENRAGE THAT WE ARE OBEYING THE EVIL GENERAL ESTEBAN!
FLEE!
RUN AWAY!
GREAT JUMPIN' JEHOSOPHAT!!!
CAPTAIN SHANTON--IT'S THE PRESIDENT! BRONCO-BUSTING A GIANT JAGUAR!
WHO ELSE WOULD YOU EXPECT TO COME THUNDERING DOWN A MOUNTAIN LIKE THAT?
COME BACK, COWARDS! IT IS ONLY A STATUE! YOU ARE SPOILING MY PLANS TO DOMINATE WORLD TRADE!
MR. PRESIDENT, ARE YOU ALL RIGHT, SIR?
YES, GEORGE, BUT THIS JAGUAR IS ABOUT TO CAUSE A BIG MESS!
NOT HOUSE-BROKEN, SIR?
WHEN CONGRESS LEARNS THIS TREASURE WAS FOUND ON LAND LEASED TO AMERICA, THEY MIGHT WANT TO KEEP IT TO FUND THE CANAL PROJECT!
FRANCE MIGHT EVEN SAY THIS TEMPLE IS NOT INCLUDED IN MY DIGGING RIGHTS!
AND EVERY NATION WHOSE CULTURE CONTRIBUTED TO THE TREASURE WILL DEMAND THEIR SHARE! THIS WILL THREATEN THE PEACE OF NORTH AND SOUTH AMERICA!
THERE'S ONLY ONE THING YOU CAN DO, T.R.!

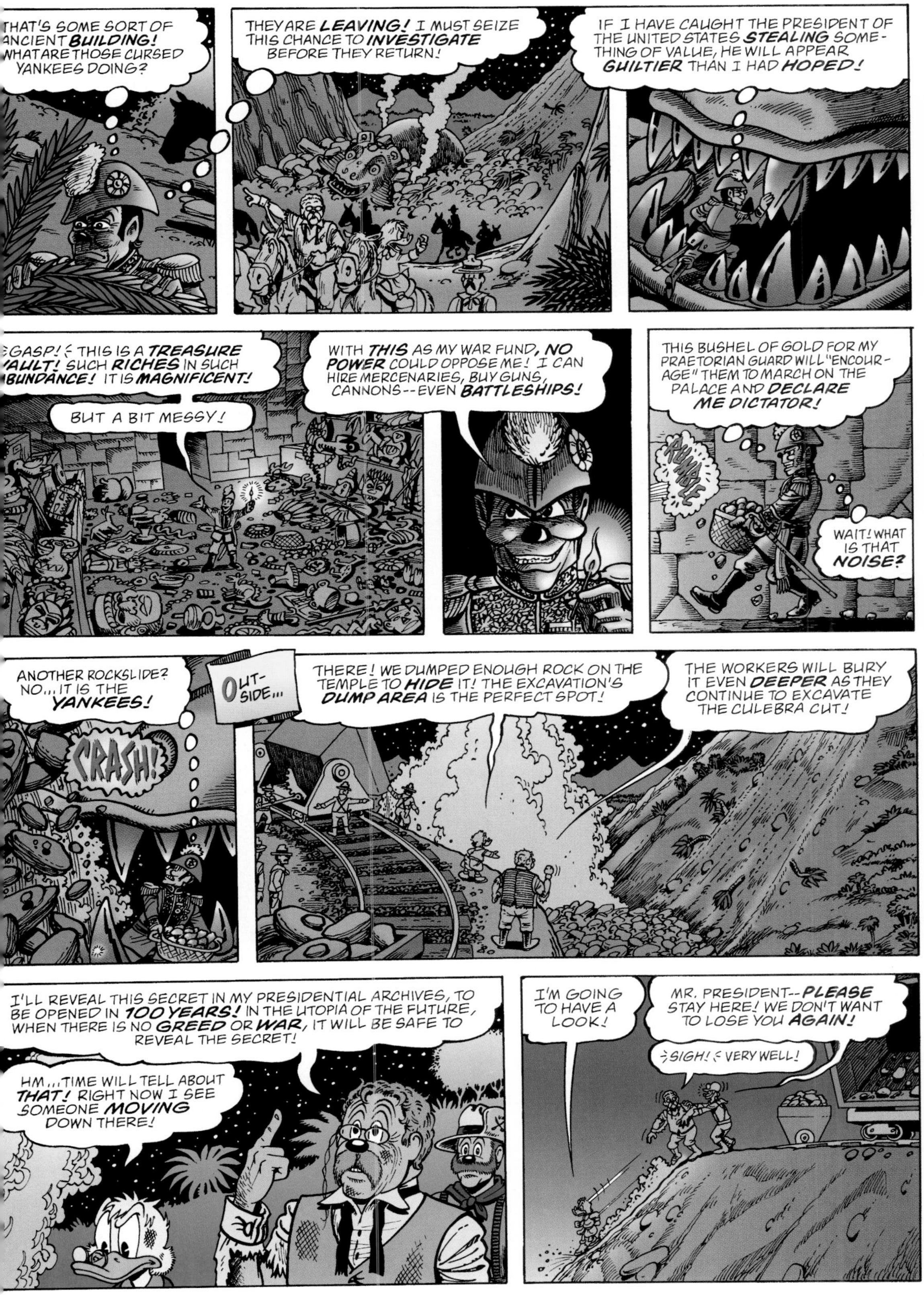
THAT'S SOME SORT OF ANCIENT BUILDING! WHAT ARE THOSE CURSED YANKEES DOING?
THEY ARE LEAVING! I MUST SEIZE THIS CHANCE TO INVESTIGATE BEFORE THEY RETURN!
IF I HAVE CAUGHT THE PRESIDENT OF THE UNITED STATES STEALING SOMETHING OF VALUE, HE WILL APPEAR GUILTIER THAN I HAD HOPED!
GASP! THIS IS A TREASURE VAULT! SUCH RICHES IN SUCH ABUNDANCE! IT IS MAGNIFICENT!
BUT A BIT MESSY!
WITH THIS AS MY WAR FUND, NO POWER COULD OPPOSE ME! I CAN HIRE MERCENARIES, BUY GUNS, CANNONS -- EVEN BATTLESHIPS!
THIS BUSHEL OF GOLD FOR MY PRAETORIAN GUARD WILL "ENCOURAGE" THEM TO MARCH ON THE PALACE AND DECLARE ME DICTATOR!
RUMBLE
WAIT! WHAT IS THAT NOISE?
ANOTHER ROCKSLIDE? NO... IT IS THE YANKEES!
CRASH!
OUTSIDE...
THERE! WE DUMPED ENOUGH ROCK ON THE TEMPLE TO HIDE IT! THE EXCAVATION'S DUMP AREA IS THE PERFECT SPOT!
THE WORKERS WILL BURY IT EVEN DEEPER AS THEY CONTINUE TO EXCAVATE THE CULEBRA CUT!
I'LL REVEAL THIS SECRET IN MY PRESIDENTIAL ARCHIVES, TO BE OPENED IN 100 YEARS! IN THE UTOPIA OF THE FUTURE, WHEN THERE IS NO GREED OR WAR, IT WILL BE SAFE TO REVEAL THE SECRET!
HM... TIME WILL TELL ABOUT THAT! RIGHT NOW I SEE SOMEONE MOVING DOWN THERE!
I'M GOING TO HAVE A LOOK!
MR. PRESIDENT-- PLEASE STAY HERE! WE DON'T WANT TO LOSE YOU AGAIN!
SIGH! VERY WELL!

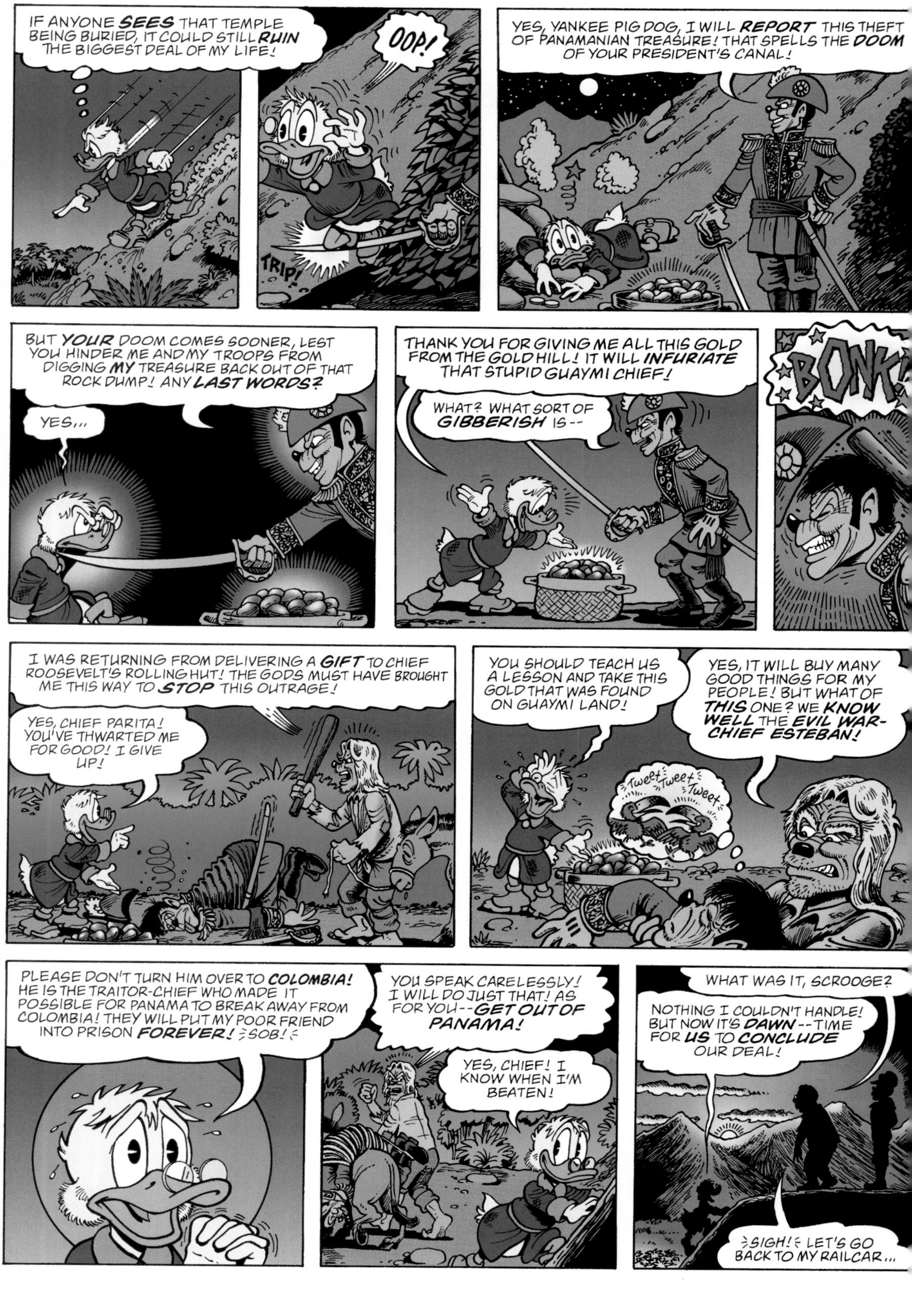
IF ANYONE SEES THAT TEMPLE BEING BURIED, IT COULD STILL RUIN THE BIGGEST DEAL OF MY LIFE!
OOP!
TRIP!
YES, YANKEE PIG DOG, I WILL REPORT THIS THEFT OF PANAMANIAN TREASURE! THAT SPELLS THE DOOM OF YOUR PRESIDENT'S CANAL!
BUT YOUR DOOM COMES SOONER, LEST YOU HINDER ME AND MY TROOPS FROM DIGGING MY TREASURE BACK OUT OF THAT ROCK DUMP! ANY LAST WORDS?
YES...
THANK YOU FOR GIVING ME ALL THIS GOLD FROM THE GOLD HILL! IT WILL INFURIATE THAT STUPID GUAYMI CHIEF!
WHAT? WHAT SORT OF GIBBERISH IS --
BONK!
I WAS RETURNING FROM DELIVERING A GIFT TO CHIEF ROOSEVELT'S ROLLING HUT! THE GODS MUST HAVE BROUGHT ME THIS WAY TO STOP THIS OUTRAGE!
YES, CHIEF PARITA! YOU'VE THWARTED ME FOR GOOD! I GIVE UP!
YOU SHOULD TEACH US A LESSON AND TAKE THIS GOLD THAT WAS FOUND ON GUAYMI LAND!
YES, IT WILL BUY MANY GOOD THINGS FOR MY PEOPLE! BUT WHAT OF THIS ONE? WE KNOW WELL THE EVIL WAR-CHIEF ESTEBAN!
Tweet Tweet Tweet
PLEASE DON'T TURN HIM OVER TO COLOMBIA! HE IS THE TRAITOR-CHIEF WHO MADE IT POSSIBLE FOR PANAMA TO BREAK AWAY FROM COLOMBIA! THEY WILL PUT MY POOR FRIEND INTO PRISON FOREVER! SOB!
YOU SPEAK CARELESSLY! I WILL DO JUST THAT! AS FOR YOU--GET OUT OF PANAMA!
YES, CHIEF! I KNOW WHEN I'M BEATEN!
WHAT WAS IT, SCROOGE?
NOTHING I COULDN'T HANDLE! BUT NOW IT'S DAWN--TIME FOR US TO CONCLUDE OUR DEAL!
SIGH! LET'S GO BACK TO MY RAILCAR...

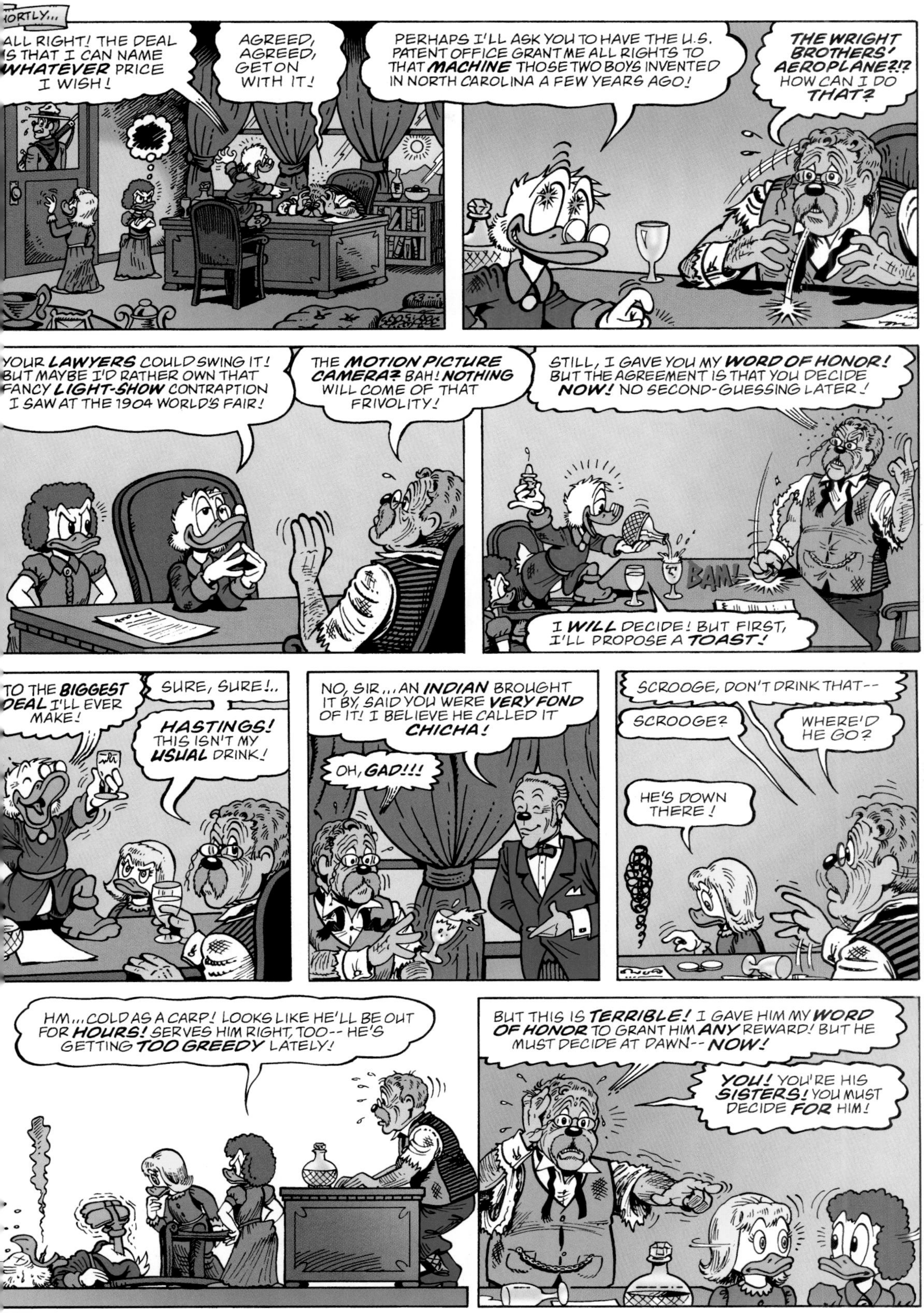

HORTLY...
ALL RIGHT! THE DEAL S THAT I CAN NAME WHATEVER PRICE I WISH!
AGREED, AGREED, GET ON WITH IT!
PERHAPS I'LL ASK YOU TO HAVE THE U.S. PATENT OFFICE GRANT ME ALL RIGHTS TO THAT MACHINE THOSE TWO BOYS INVENTED IN NORTH CAROLINA A FEW YEARS AGO!
THE WRIGHT BROTHERS' AEROPLANE?!? HOW CAN I DO THAT?
YOUR LAWYERS COULD SWING IT! BUT MAYBE I'D RATHER OWN THAT FANCY LIGHT-SHOW CONTRAPTION I SAW AT THE 1904 WORLD'S FAIR!
THE MOTION PICTURE CAMERA? BAH! NOTHING WILL COME OF THAT FRIVOLITY!
STILL, I GAVE YOU MY WORD OF HONOR! BUT THE AGREEMENT IS THAT YOU DECIDE NOW! NO SECOND-GUESSING LATER!
BAM!
I WILL DECIDE! BUT FIRST, I'LL PROPOSE A TOAST!
TO THE BIGGEST DEAL I'LL EVER MAKE!
SURE, SURE!..
HASTINGS! THIS ISN'T MY USUAL DRINK!
NO, SIR... AN INDIAN BROUGHT IT BY, SAID YOU WERE VERY FOND OF IT! I BELIEVE HE CALLED IT CHICHA!
OH, GAD!!!
SCROOGE, DON'T DRINK THAT--
SCROOGE?
WHERE'D HE GO?
HE'S DOWN THERE!
HM... COLD AS A CARP! LOOKS LIKE HE'LL BE OUT FOR HOURS! SERVES HIM RIGHT, TOO-- HE'S GETTING TOO GREEDY LATELY!
BUT THIS IS TERRIBLE! I GAVE HIM MY WORD OF HONOR TO GRANT HIM ANY REWARD! BUT HE MUST DECIDE AT DAWN-- NOW!
YOU! YOU'RE HIS SISTERS! YOU MUST DECIDE FOR HIM!

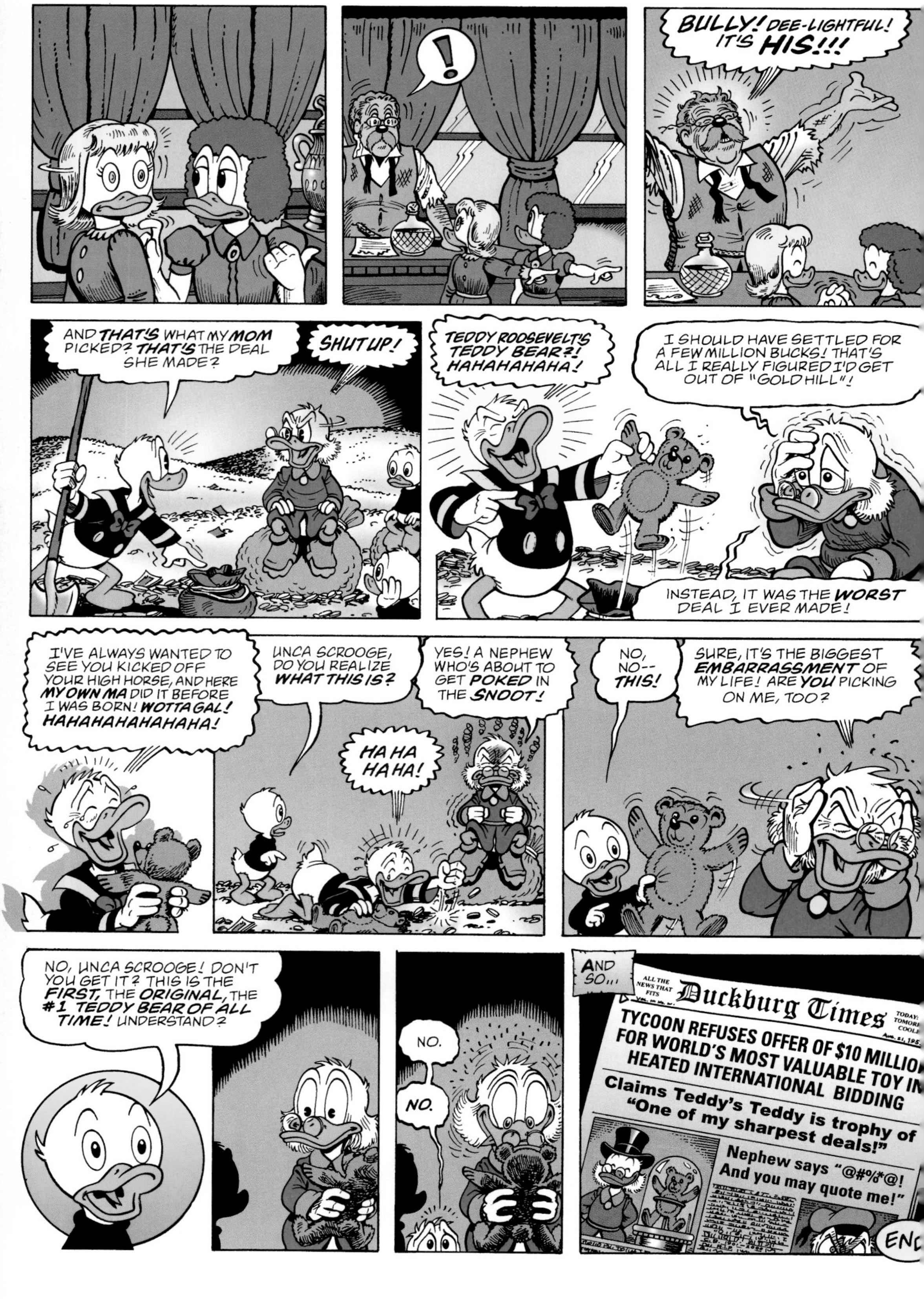
!
BULLY! DEE-LIGHTFUL! IT'S HIS!!!
AND THAT'S WHAT MY MOM PICKED? THAT'S THE DEAL SHE MADE?
SHUT UP!
TEDDY ROOSEVELT'S TEDDY BEAR?! HAHAHAHAHA!
I SHOULD HAVE SETTLED FOR A FEW MILLION BUCKS! THAT'S ALL I REALLY FIGURED I'D GET OUT OF "GOLD HILL"!
INSTEAD, IT WAS THE WORST DEAL I EVER MADE!
I'VE ALWAYS WANTED TO SEE YOU KICKED OFF YOUR HIGH HORSE, AND HERE MY OWN MA DID IT BEFORE I WAS BORN! WOTTA GAL! HAHAHAHAHAHAHA!
UNCA SCROOGE, DO YOU REALIZE WHAT THIS IS?
YES! A NEPHEW WHO'S ABOUT TO GET POKED IN THE SNOOT!
HA HA HA HA!
NO, NO-- THIS!
SURE, IT'S THE BIGGEST EMBARRASSMENT OF MY LIFE! ARE YOU PICKING ON ME, TOO?
NO, UNCA SCROOGE! DON'T YOU GET IT? THIS IS THE FIRST, THE ORIGINAL, THE #1 TEDDY BEAR OF ALL TIME! UNDERSTAND?
NO.
NO.
AND SO...
ALL THE NEWS THAT FITS
Duckburg Times
TYCOON REFUSES OFFER OF $10 MILLIO
FOR WORLD'S MOST VALUABLE TOY IN
HEATED INTERNATIONAL BIDDING
Claims Teddy's Teddy is trophy of
"One of my sharpest deals!"
Nephew says "@#%*@!
And you may quote me!"
END

MORE DISNEY excitement TO COME!

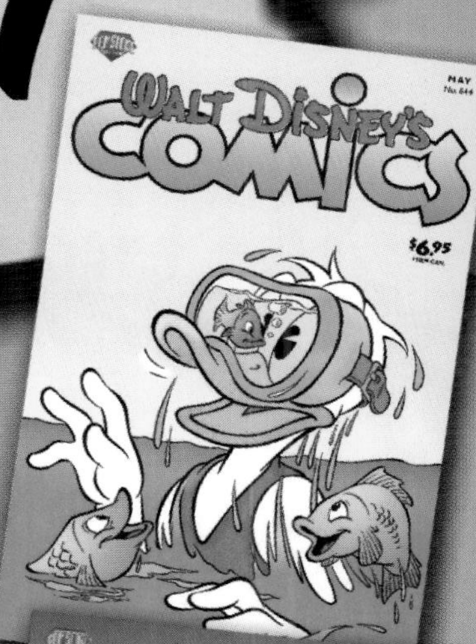
MAY No. 644
WALT DISNEY'S COMICS
$6.95

If you like this comic, you'll want to be on board for all the fun in the months to come, with Gemstone Publishing's exciting line of Disney comic books.

For collectors: Walt Disney's Comics and Stories and Uncle Scrooge, providing the best of vintage and recent classic tales by such highly-acclaimed creators as Carl Barks, Pat Block, Daniel Branca, Cesar Ferioli, David Gerstein, Michael T. Gilbert, Daan Jippes, Don Markstein, Pat McGreal, Dave Rawson, Don Rosa, Noel Van Horn, William Van Horn, and many more. These books are 64 pages and in the sturdy, squarebound prestige format that collectors love.

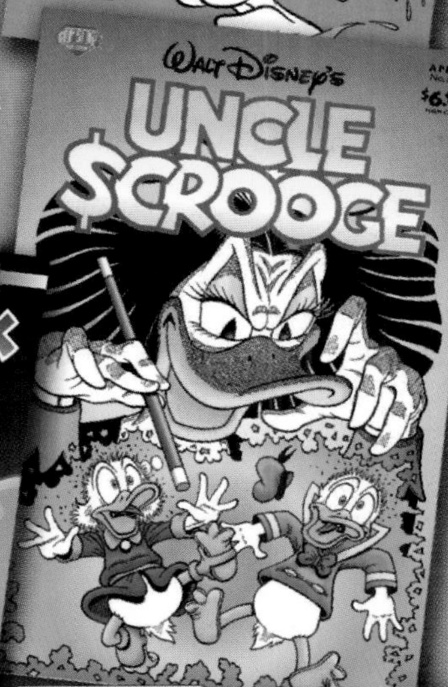
WALT DISNEY'S
APRIL
$6.95
UNCLE SCROOGE

For readers on the go: Donald Duck Adventures, the first title in our new 5" X 7½" "Take-Along Comic" series, gives you long adventure stories starring Mickey, Donald, Scrooge, and others in modern stories that take them beyond the limits of space and time.

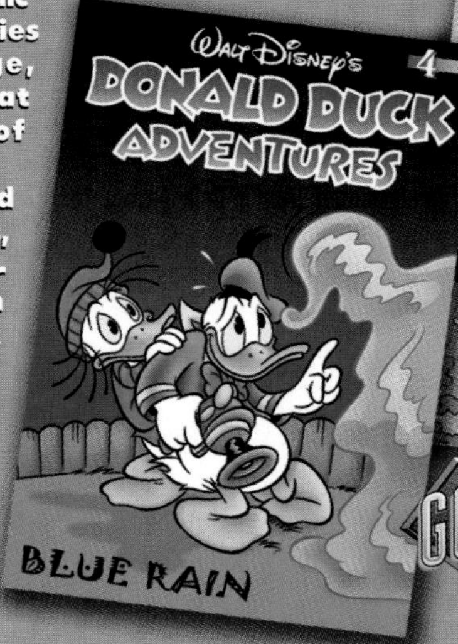
WALT DISNEY'S
4
DONALD DUCK ADVENTURES
BLUE RAIN

For readers of all ages: Donald Duck and Mickey Mouse and Friends, offering Disney fans the best contemporary Mouse and Duck stories in the familiar 32-page, stapled, comic book format.

Look for them at your local comic shop! Can't find a comic shop? Try the Toll Free Comic Shop Locator Service at (888) COMIC BOOK for the shop nearest you! If you can't find Gemstone's Disney comics in your neighborhood you may subscribe at no extra charge, and we'll pay the postage! Use the coupon below, or a copy:

GEMSTONE PUBLISHING

Mail this coupon to: Gemstone Publishing, P.O. Box 469, West Plains, Missouri 65775.
MO residents add 6.975% sales tax; MD residents add 5% sales tax.

❒ Walt Disney's Comics and Stories: $83.40 for 12 issues ($90.00 Canada, payable in US funds)

❒ Walt Disney's Uncle Scrooge: $83.40 for 12 issues ($90.00 Canada, payable in US funds)

❒ Walt Disney's Donald Duck and Friends: $35.40 for 12 issues ($40.00 Canada, payable in US funds)

❒ Walt Disney's Mickey Mouse and Friends: $35.40 for 12 issues ($40.00 Canada, payable in US funds)

❒ D.D.A.: $95.40 for 12 issues ($105.00 Canada, payable in US funds)

Name: ______________________

Address: ______________________

City: ______________ State: ________ Zip Code: ________

Email: ______________________

❒ Visa ❒ MasterCard ❒ Other Card # ______________ Exp. Date: ________

COMIC SHOP LOCATOR SERVICE
888-COMIC-BOOK
888-266-4226

www.gemstonepub.com/disney

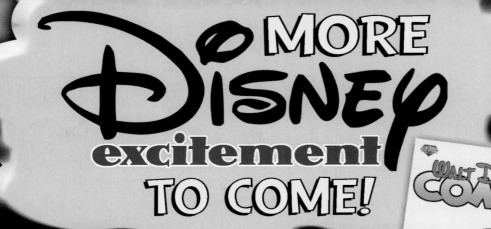

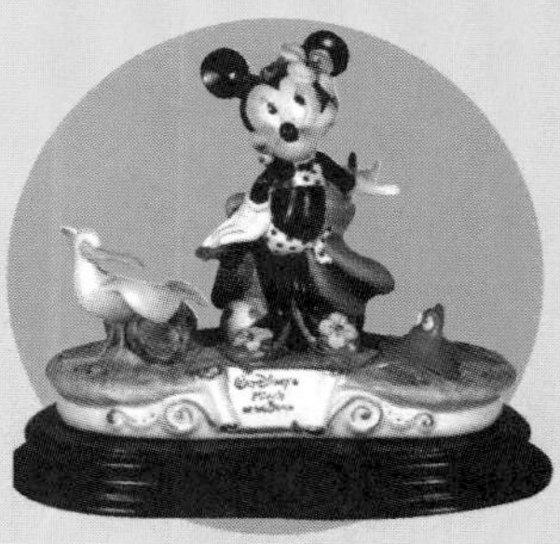
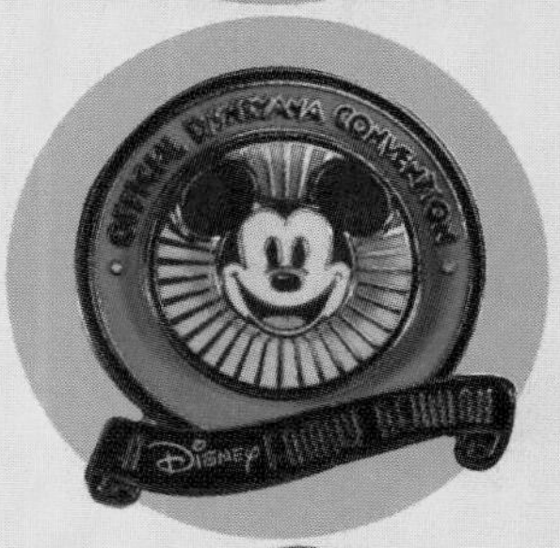
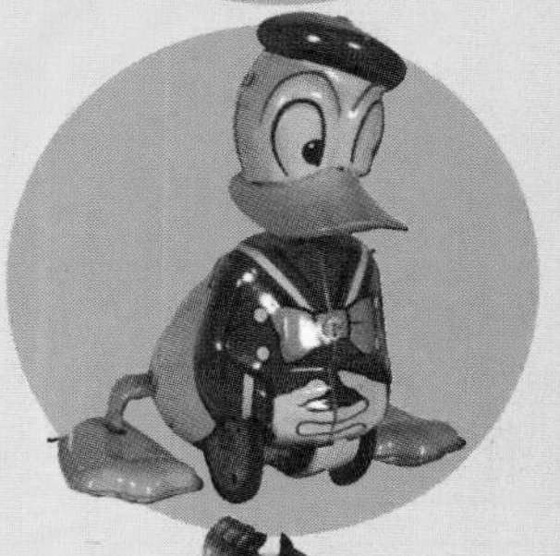
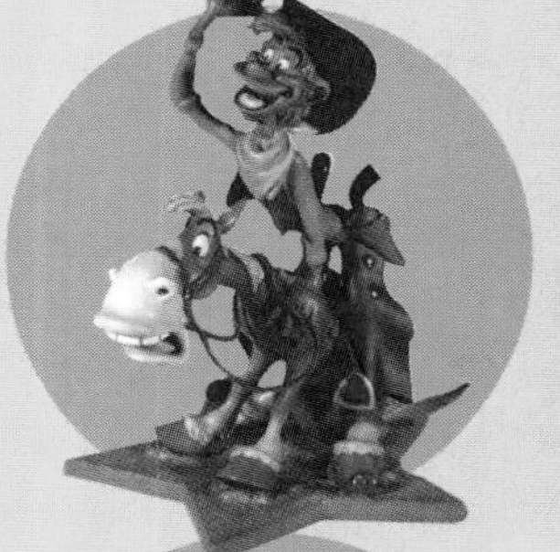
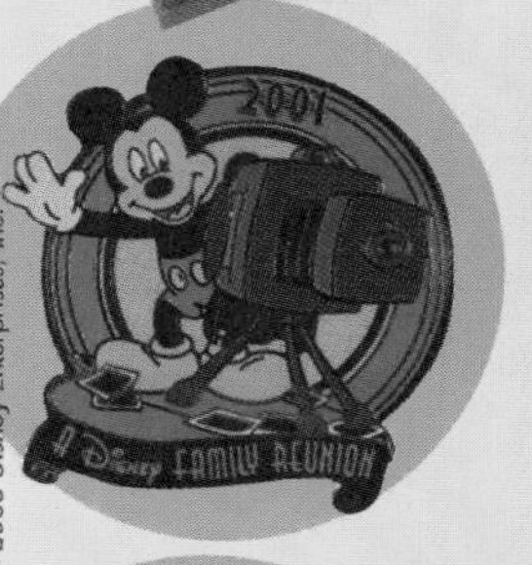

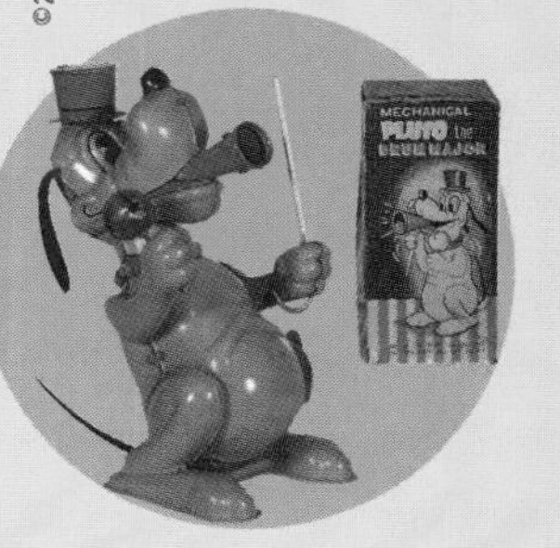

How much is your collection worth?

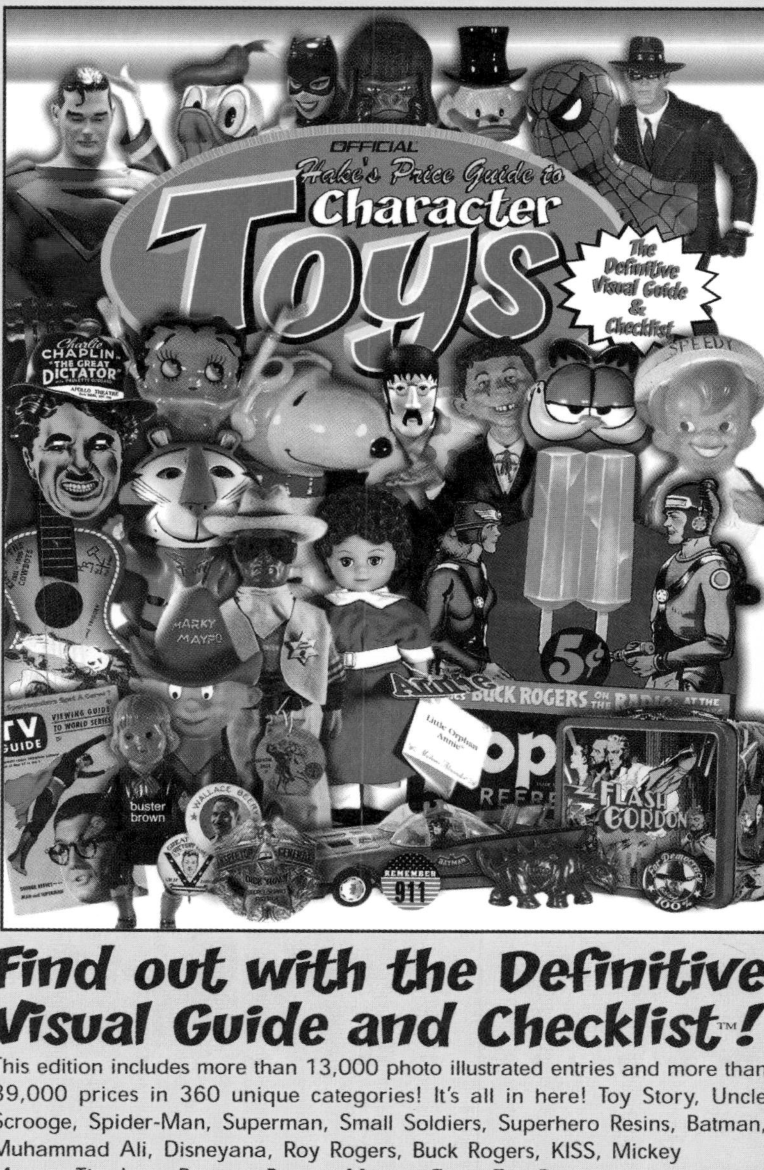
OFFICIAL
Hake's Price Guide to
Character
Toys
The Definitive Visual Guide & Checklist

Find out with the Definitive Visual Guide and Checklist™!

This edition includes more than 13,000 photo illustrated entries and more than 39,000 prices in 360 unique categories! It's all in here! Toy Story, Uncle Scrooge, Spider-Man, Superman, Small Soldiers, Superhero Resins, Batman, Muhammad Ali, Disneyana, Roy Rogers, Buck Rogers, KISS, Mickey Mouse, The Lone Ranger, Puppet Master, Elvis, The Phantom, X-Men, Charlie Chaplin, The Cisco Kid, Donald Duck, Captain Marvel, Laurel & Hardy, Howdy Doody, Planet of the Apes, MAD, Hopalong Cassidy, Captain America, Toy Guns and more!

$35 (+s&h)

Available at your local comic book shop. Can't find a comic shop near you? Try the Toll Free Comic Shop Locator Service at (888) COMIC BOOK. Or you can order direct from Gemstone Publishing by calling Toll Free (888) 375-9800 ext. 249.

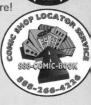

COMIC SHOP LOCATOR SERVICE
888-COMIC-BOOK
888-266-4226

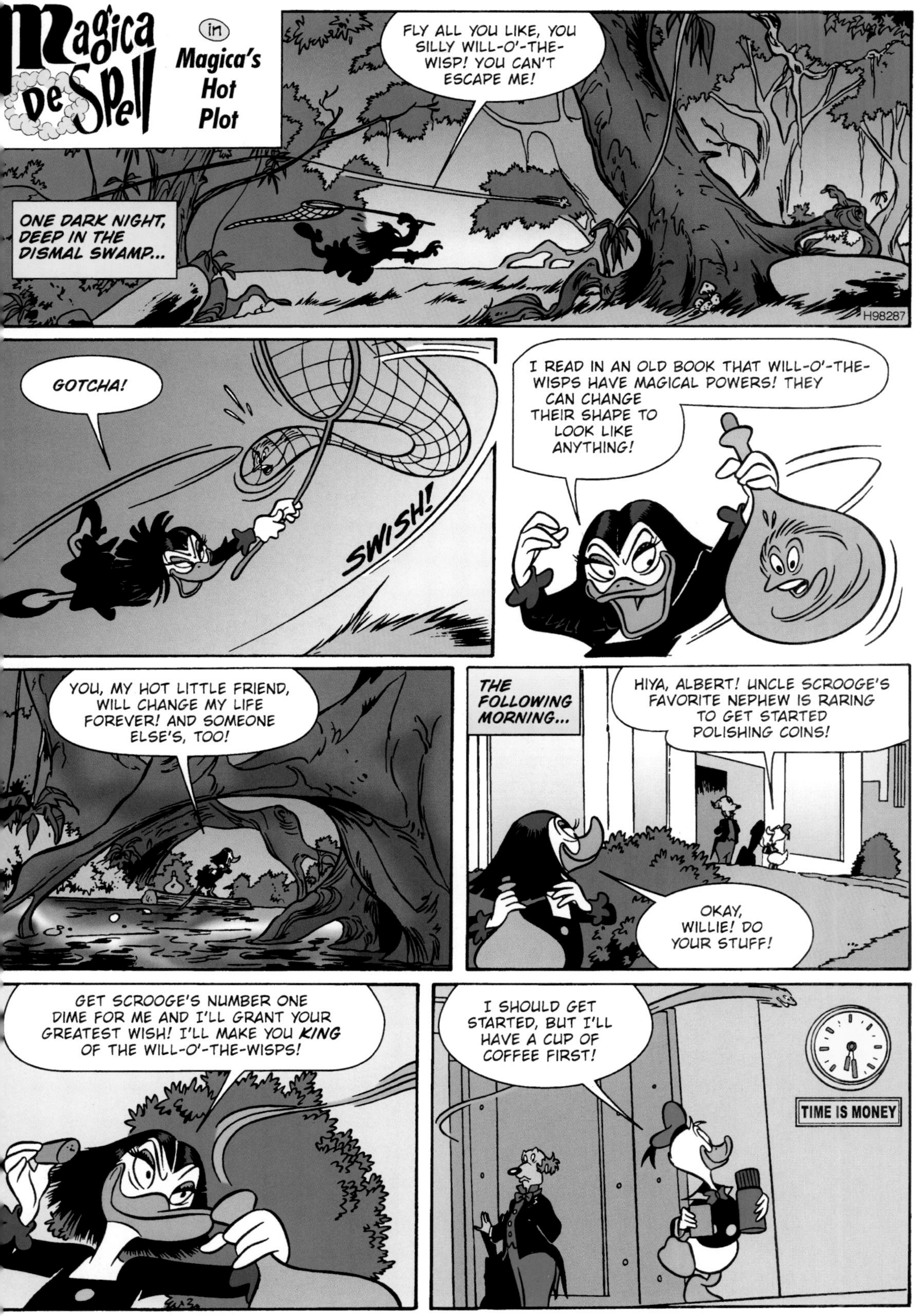
Magica De Spell
in
Magica's Hot Plot
FLY ALL YOU LIKE, YOU SILLY WILL-O'-THE-WISP! YOU CAN'T ESCAPE ME!
ONE DARK NIGHT, DEEP IN THE DISMAL SWAMP...
H98287
GOTCHA!
SWISH!
I READ IN AN OLD BOOK THAT WILL-O'-THE-WISPS HAVE MAGICAL POWERS! THEY CAN CHANGE THEIR SHAPE TO LOOK LIKE ANYTHING!
YOU, MY HOT LITTLE FRIEND, WILL CHANGE MY LIFE FOREVER! AND SOMEONE ELSE'S, TOO!
THE FOLLOWING MORNING...
HIYA, ALBERT! UNCLE SCROOGE'S FAVORITE NEPHEW IS RARING TO GET STARTED POLISHING COINS!
OKAY, WILLIE! DO YOUR STUFF!
GET SCROOGE'S NUMBER ONE DIME FOR ME AND I'LL GRANT YOUR GREATEST WISH! I'LL MAKE YOU KING OF THE WILL-O'-THE-WISPS!
I SHOULD GET STARTED, BUT I'LL HAVE A CUP OF COFFEE FIRST!
TIME IS MONEY

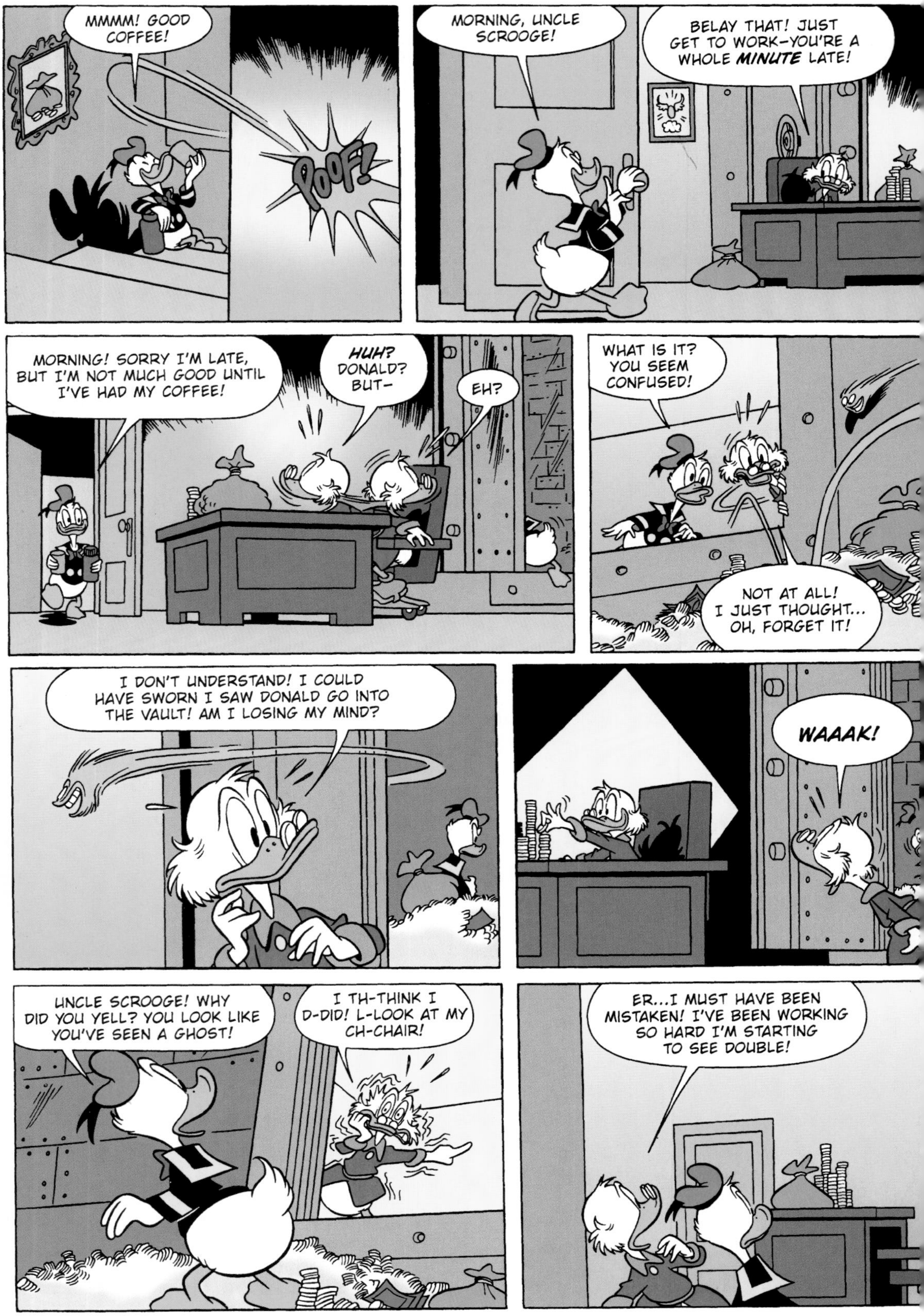
MMMM! GOOD COFFEE!
POOF!
MORNING, UNCLE SCROOGE!
BELAY THAT! JUST GET TO WORK–YOU'RE A WHOLE *MINUTE* LATE!
MORNING! SORRY I'M LATE, BUT I'M NOT MUCH GOOD UNTIL I'VE HAD MY COFFEE!
HUH? DONALD? BUT–
EH?
WHAT IS IT? YOU SEEM CONFUSED!
NOT AT ALL! I JUST THOUGHT... OH, FORGET IT!
I DON'T UNDERSTAND! I COULD HAVE SWORN I SAW DONALD GO INTO THE VAULT! AM I LOSING MY MIND?
WAAAK!
UNCLE SCROOGE! WHY DID YOU YELL? YOU LOOK LIKE YOU'VE SEEN A GHOST!
I TH-THINK I D-DID! L-LOOK AT MY CH-CHAIR!
ER...I MUST HAVE BEEN MISTAKEN! I'VE BEEN WORKING SO HARD I'M STARTING TO SEE DOUBLE!

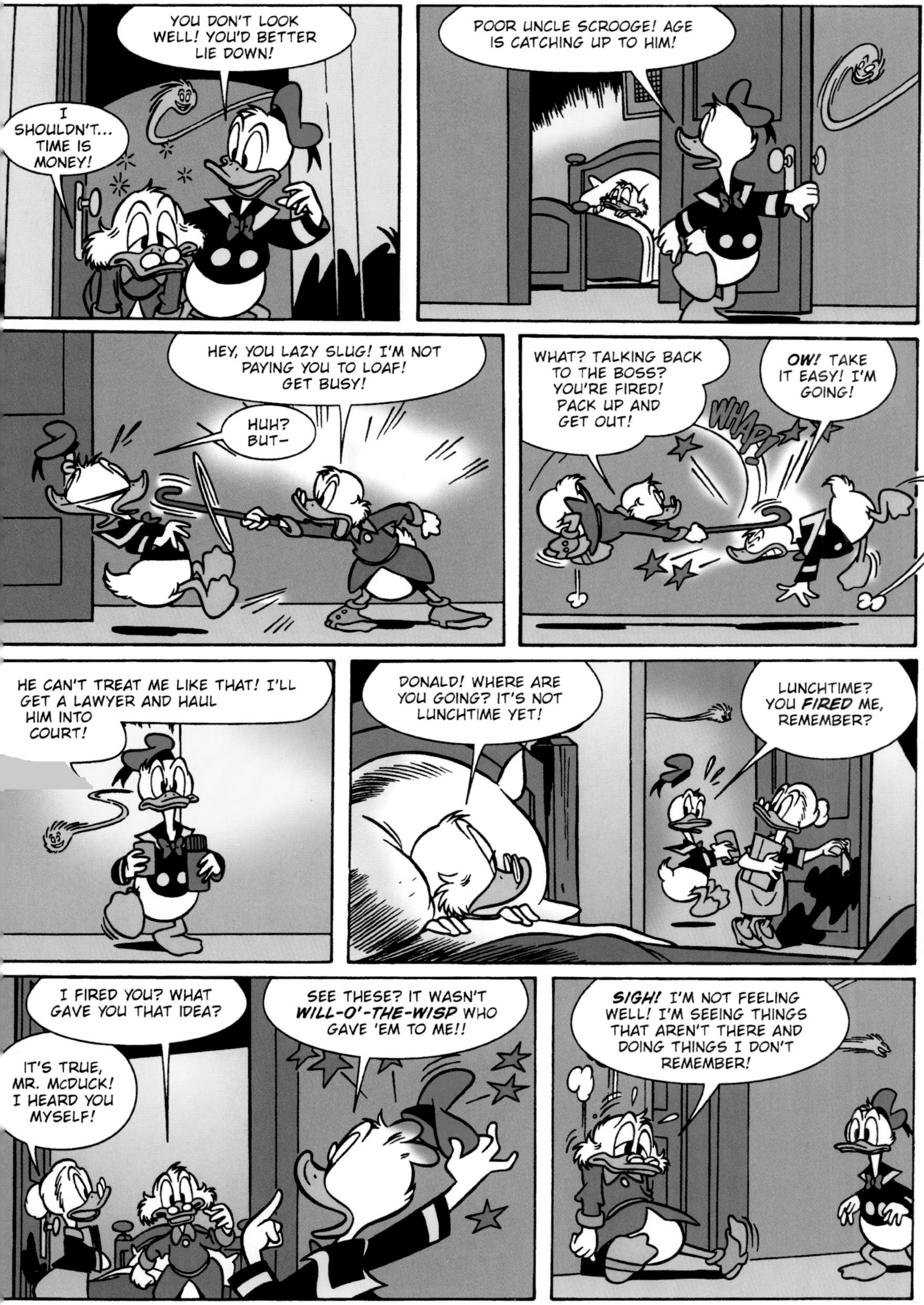
YOU DON'T LOOK WELL! YOU'D BETTER LIE DOWN!
I SHOULDN'T... TIME IS MONEY!
POOR UNCLE SCROOGE! AGE IS CATCHING UP TO HIM!
HEY, YOU LAZY SLUG! I'M NOT PAYING YOU TO LOAF! GET BUSY!
HUH? BUT–
WHAT? TALKING BACK TO THE BOSS? YOU'RE FIRED! PACK UP AND GET OUT!
WHAP!
OW! TAKE IT EASY! I'M GOING!
HE CAN'T TREAT ME LIKE THAT! I'LL GET A LAWYER AND HAUL HIM INTO COURT!
DONALD! WHERE ARE YOU GOING? IT'S NOT LUNCHTIME YET!
LUNCHTIME? YOU FIRED ME, REMEMBER?
I FIRED YOU? WHAT GAVE YOU THAT IDEA?
IT'S TRUE, MR. McDUCK! I HEARD YOU MYSELF!
SEE THESE? IT WASN'T WILL-O'-THE-WISP WHO GAVE 'EM TO ME!!
SIGH! I'M NOT FEELING WELL! I'M SEEING THINGS THAT AREN'T THERE AND DOING THINGS I DON'T REMEMBER!

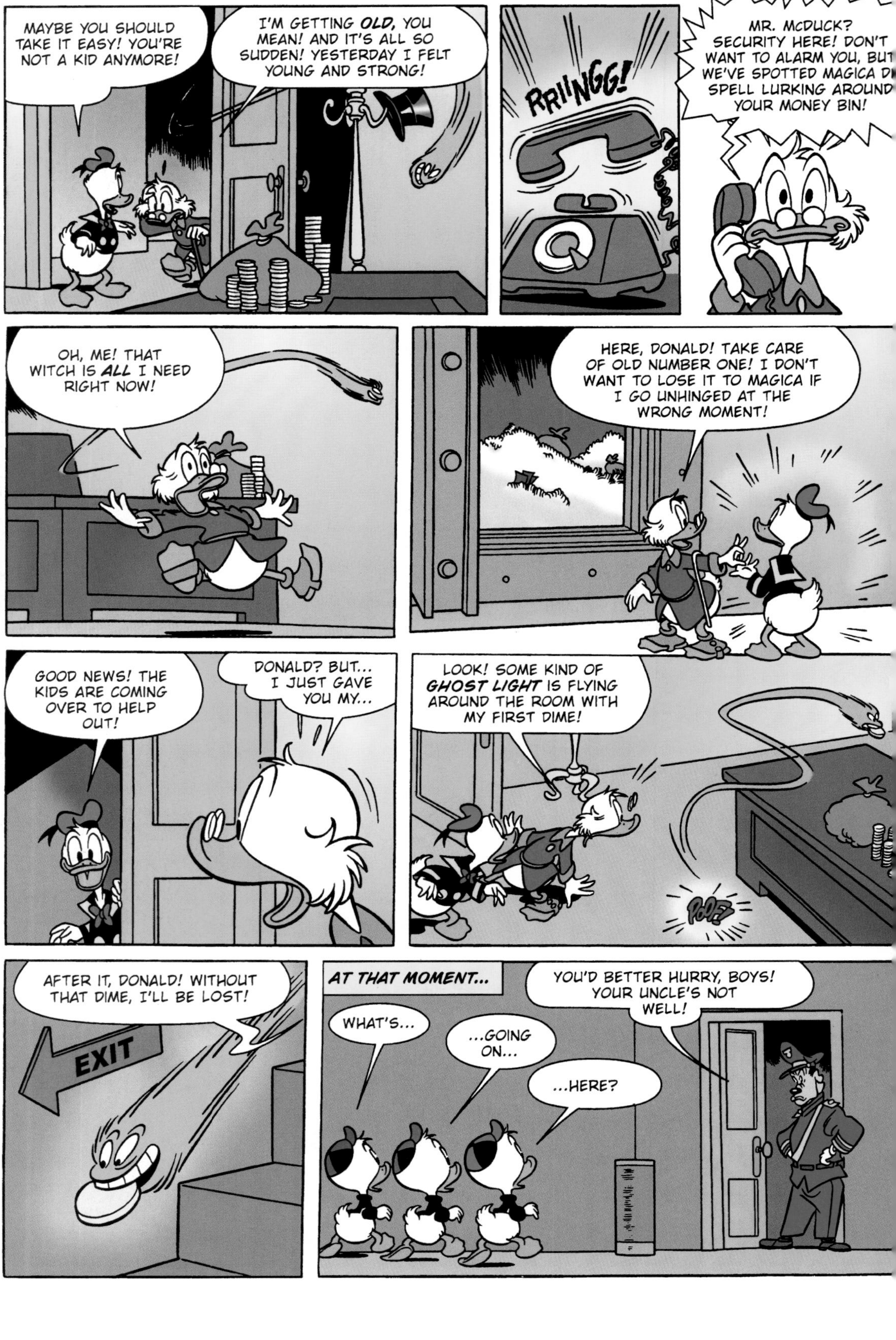
MAYBE YOU SHOULD TAKE IT EASY! YOU'RE NOT A KID ANYMORE!
I'M GETTING OLD, YOU MEAN! AND IT'S ALL SO SUDDEN! YESTERDAY I FELT YOUNG AND STRONG!
RRIINGG!
MR. McDUCK? SECURITY HERE! DON'T WANT TO ALARM YOU, BUT WE'VE SPOTTED MAGICA DE SPELL LURKING AROUND YOUR MONEY BIN!
OH, ME! THAT WITCH IS ALL I NEED RIGHT NOW!
HERE, DONALD! TAKE CARE OF OLD NUMBER ONE! I DON'T WANT TO LOSE IT TO MAGICA IF I GO UNHINGED AT THE WRONG MOMENT!
GOOD NEWS! THE KIDS ARE COMING OVER TO HELP OUT!
DONALD? BUT... I JUST GAVE YOU MY...
LOOK! SOME KIND OF GHOST LIGHT IS FLYING AROUND THE ROOM WITH MY FIRST DIME!
POOF!
AFTER IT, DONALD! WITHOUT THAT DIME, I'LL BE LOST!
EXIT
AT THAT MOMENT...
YOU'D BETTER HURRY, BOYS! YOUR UNCLE'S NOT WELL!
WHAT'S...
...GOING ON...
...HERE?

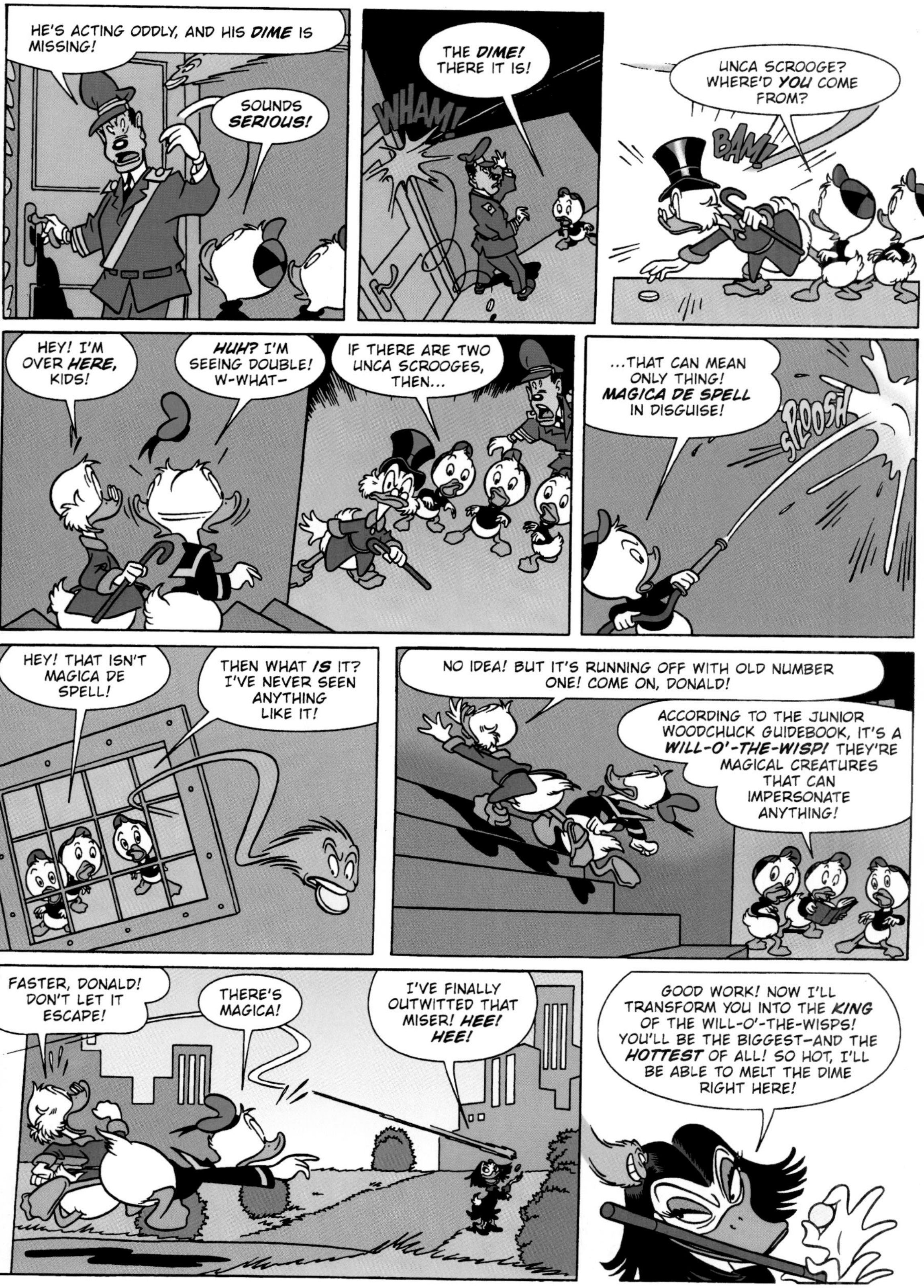
HE'S ACTING ODDLY, AND HIS DIME IS MISSING!
SOUNDS SERIOUS!
THE DIME! THERE IT IS!
WHAM!
UNCA SCROOGE? WHERE'D YOU COME FROM?
BAM!
HEY! I'M OVER HERE, KIDS!
HUH? I'M SEEING DOUBLE! W-WHAT-
IF THERE ARE TWO UNCA SCROOGES, THEN...
...THAT CAN MEAN ONLY THING! MAGICA DE SPELL IN DISGUISE!
SPLOOSH
HEY! THAT ISN'T MAGICA DE SPELL!
THEN WHAT IS IT? I'VE NEVER SEEN ANYTHING LIKE IT!
NO IDEA! BUT IT'S RUNNING OFF WITH OLD NUMBER ONE! COME ON, DONALD!
ACCORDING TO THE JUNIOR WOODCHUCK GUIDEBOOK, IT'S A WILL-O'-THE-WISP! THEY'RE MAGICAL CREATURES THAT CAN IMPERSONATE ANYTHING!
FASTER, DONALD! DON'T LET IT ESCAPE!
THERE'S MAGICA!
I'VE FINALLY OUTWITTED THAT MISER! HEE! HEE!
GOOD WORK! NOW I'LL TRANSFORM YOU INTO THE KING OF THE WILL-O'-THE-WISPS! YOU'LL BE THE BIGGEST—AND THE HOTTEST OF ALL! SO HOT, I'LL BE ABLE TO MELT THE DIME RIGHT HERE!

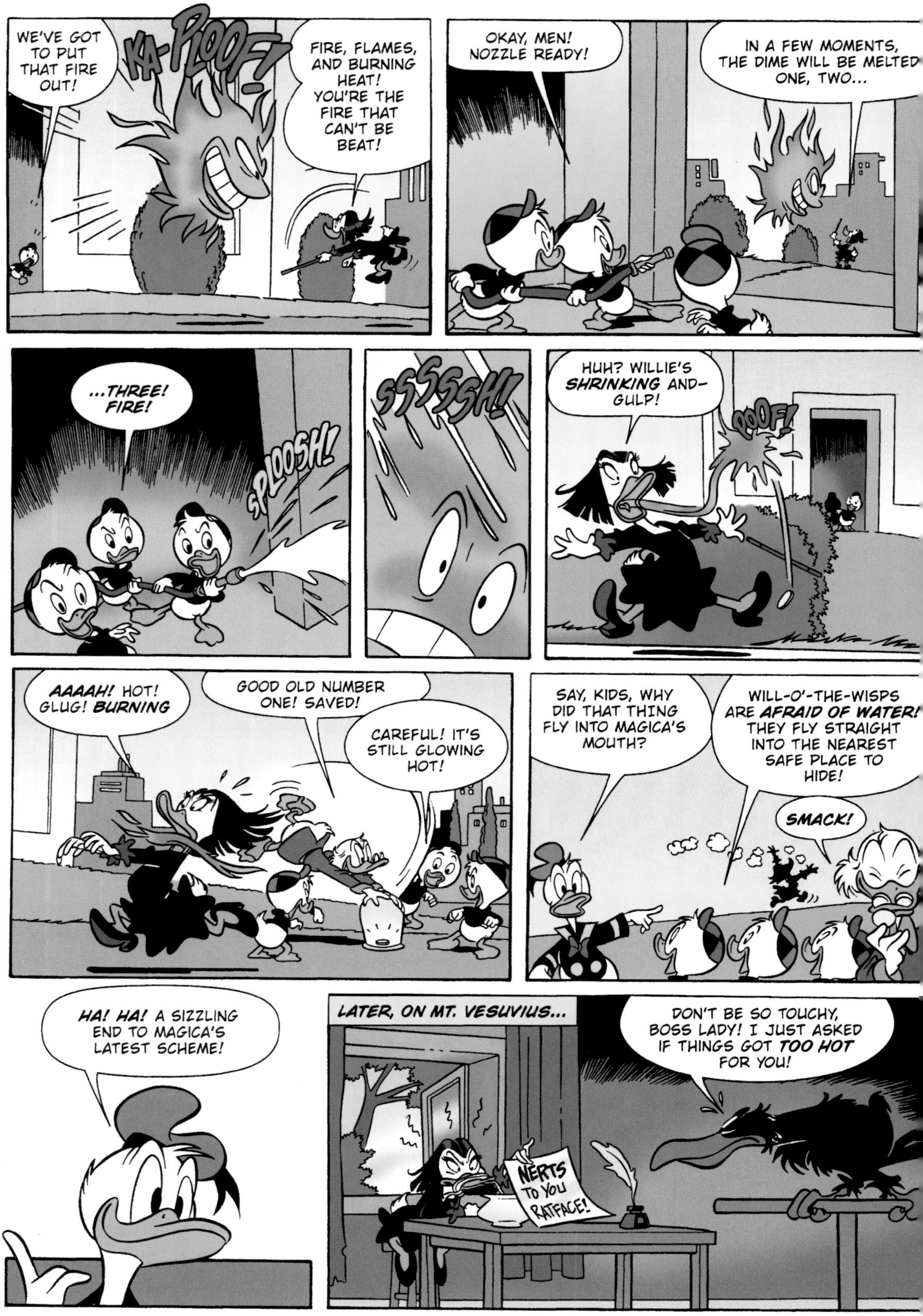

WE'VE GOT TO PUT THAT FIRE OUT!
KA-PLOOF!
FIRE, FLAMES, AND BURNING HEAT! YOU'RE THE FIRE THAT CAN'T BE BEAT!
OKAY, MEN! NOZZLE READY!
IN A FEW MOMENTS, THE DIME WILL BE MELTED! ONE, TWO...
...THREE! FIRE!
SPLOOSH!
SSSSSH!
HUH? WILLIE'S SHRINKING AND– GULP!
POOF!
AAAAH! HOT! GLUG! BURNING
GOOD OLD NUMBER ONE! SAVED!
CAREFUL! IT'S STILL GLOWING HOT!
SAY, KIDS, WHY DID THAT THING FLY INTO MAGICA'S MOUTH?
WILL-O'-THE-WISPS ARE AFRAID OF WATER! THEY FLY STRAIGHT INTO THE NEAREST SAFE PLACE TO HIDE!
SMACK!
HA! HA! A SIZZLING END TO MAGICA'S LATEST SCHEME!
LATER, ON MT. VESUVIUS...
DON'T BE SO TOUCHY, BOSS LADY! I JUST ASKED IF THINGS GOT TOO HOT FOR YOU!
NERTS TO YOU RATFACE!

WALT DISNEY'S

GYRO GEARLOOSE in PROPHETS, GO HOME

LET THE ORACLE PREDICT YOUR FUTURE! THE ORACLE WILL REVEAL WHAT'S IN STORE FOR YOU! ONLY FIFTY CENTS!

THE ORACLE

FORTUNES TOLD 50 CENTS

FORTUNES TOLD 50 CENTS

98292

LOOK AT THAT! WHAT A NEAT PIECE OF MACHINERY!

TAKE MY HAND AND YOUR FUTURE WILL BE AN OPEN BOOK! ONLY FIFTY CENTS!

THE ORACLE

I'M CURIOUS TO SEE WHAT KIND OF PREDICTIONS THIS GADGET CAN COME UP WITH!

FORTUNES TOLD 50 CENTS

YOU WILL BE TRIUMPHANT IN THE TRIAL AHEAD! TOMORROW IS A LUCKY DAY!

WOW!

FORTUNES TOLD 50 CENTS

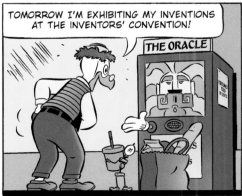

TOMORROW I'M EXHIBITING MY INVENTIONS AT THE INVENTORS' CONVENTION!

THE ORACLE

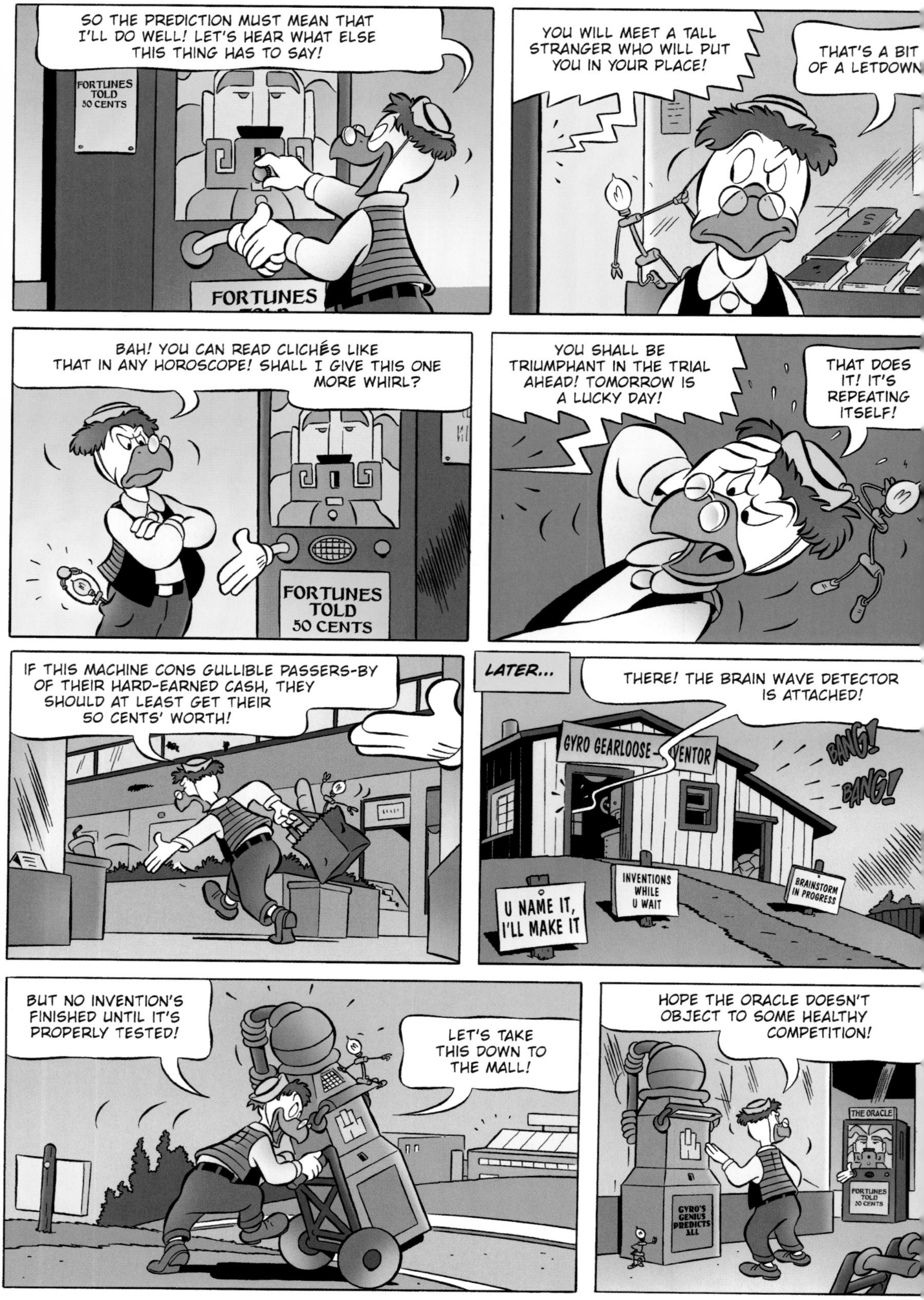
SO THE PREDICTION MUST MEAN THAT I'LL DO WELL! LET'S HEAR WHAT ELSE THIS THING HAS TO SAY!
FORTUNES TOLD 50 CENTS
FORTUNES
YOU WILL MEET A TALL STRANGER WHO WILL PUT YOU IN YOUR PLACE!
THAT'S A BIT OF A LETDOWN
BAH! YOU CAN READ CLICHÉS LIKE THAT IN ANY HOROSCOPE! SHALL I GIVE THIS ONE MORE WHIRL?
FORTUNES TOLD 50 CENTS
YOU SHALL BE TRIUMPHANT IN THE TRIAL AHEAD! TOMORROW IS A LUCKY DAY!
THAT DOES IT! IT'S REPEATING ITSELF!
IF THIS MACHINE CONS GULLIBLE PASSERS-BY OF THEIR HARD-EARNED CASH, THEY SHOULD AT LEAST GET THEIR 50 CENTS' WORTH!
LATER...
THERE! THE BRAIN WAVE DETECTOR IS ATTACHED!
GYRO GEARLOOSE-INVENTOR
BANG!
BANG!
U NAME IT, I'LL MAKE IT
INVENTIONS WHILE U WAIT
BRAINSTORM IN PROGRESS
BUT NO INVENTION'S FINISHED UNTIL IT'S PROPERLY TESTED!
LET'S TAKE THIS DOWN TO THE MALL!
HOPE THE ORACLE DOESN'T OBJECT TO SOME HEALTHY COMPETITION!
GYRO'S GENIUS PREDICTS ALL
THE ORACLE
FORTUNES TOLD 50 CENTS

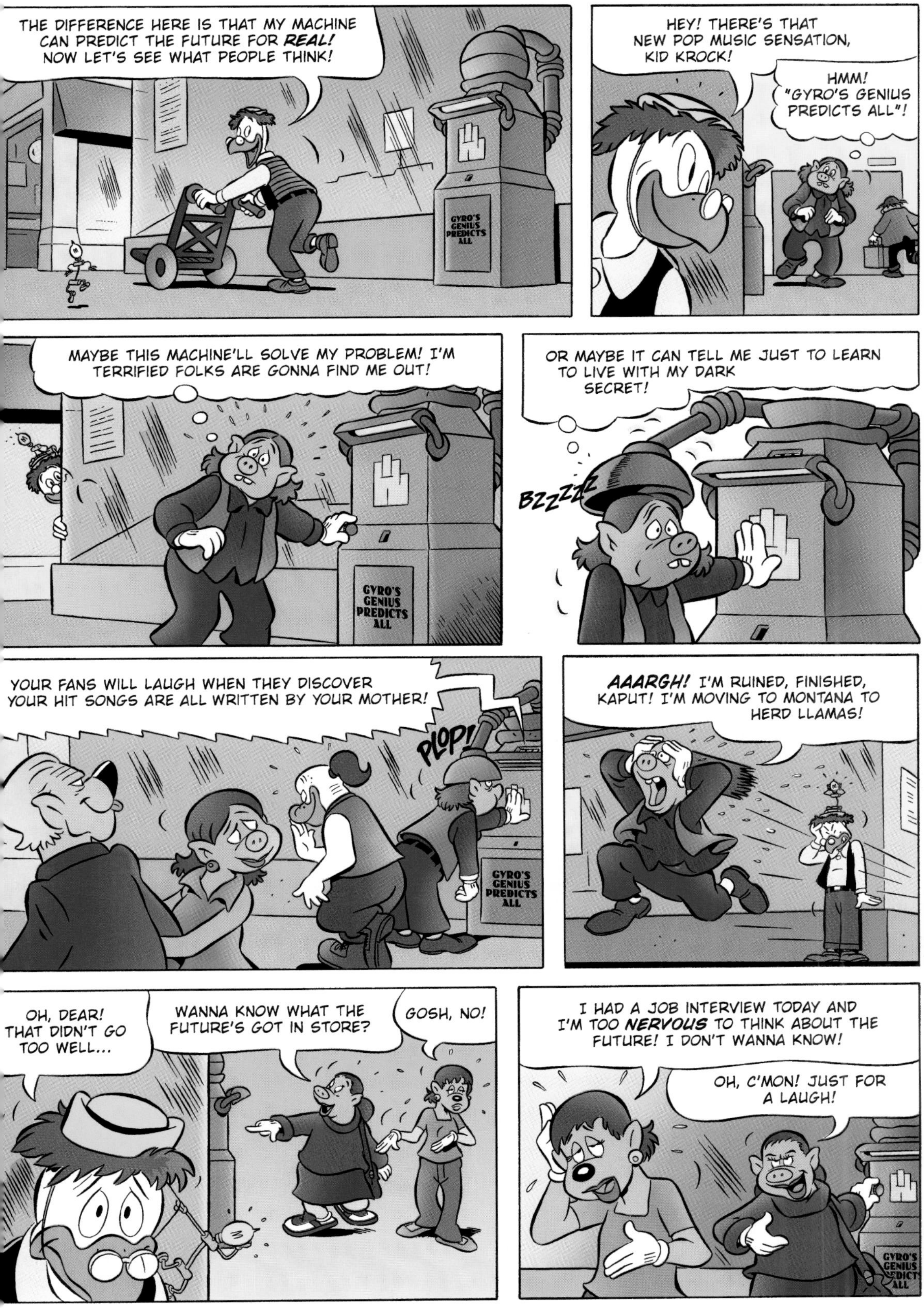
THE DIFFERENCE HERE IS THAT MY MACHINE CAN PREDICT THE FUTURE FOR REAL! NOW LET'S SEE WHAT PEOPLE THINK!
GYRO'S GENIUS PREDICTS ALL
HEY! THERE'S THAT NEW POP MUSIC SENSATION, KID KROCK!
HMM! "GYRO'S GENIUS PREDICTS ALL"!
MAYBE THIS MACHINE'LL SOLVE MY PROBLEM! I'M TERRIFIED FOLKS ARE GONNA FIND ME OUT!
GYRO'S GENIUS PREDICTS ALL
OR MAYBE IT CAN TELL ME JUST TO LEARN TO LIVE WITH MY DARK SECRET!
BZZZZZ
YOUR FANS WILL LAUGH WHEN THEY DISCOVER YOUR HIT SONGS ARE ALL WRITTEN BY YOUR MOTHER!
PLOP!
GYRO'S GENIUS PREDICTS ALL
AAARGH! I'M RUINED, FINISHED, KAPUT! I'M MOVING TO MONTANA TO HERD LLAMAS!
OH, DEAR! THAT DIDN'T GO TOO WELL...
WANNA KNOW WHAT THE FUTURE'S GOT IN STORE?
GOSH, NO!
I HAD A JOB INTERVIEW TODAY AND I'M TOO NERVOUS TO THINK ABOUT THE FUTURE! I DON'T WANNA KNOW!
OH, C'MON! JUST FOR A LAUGH!

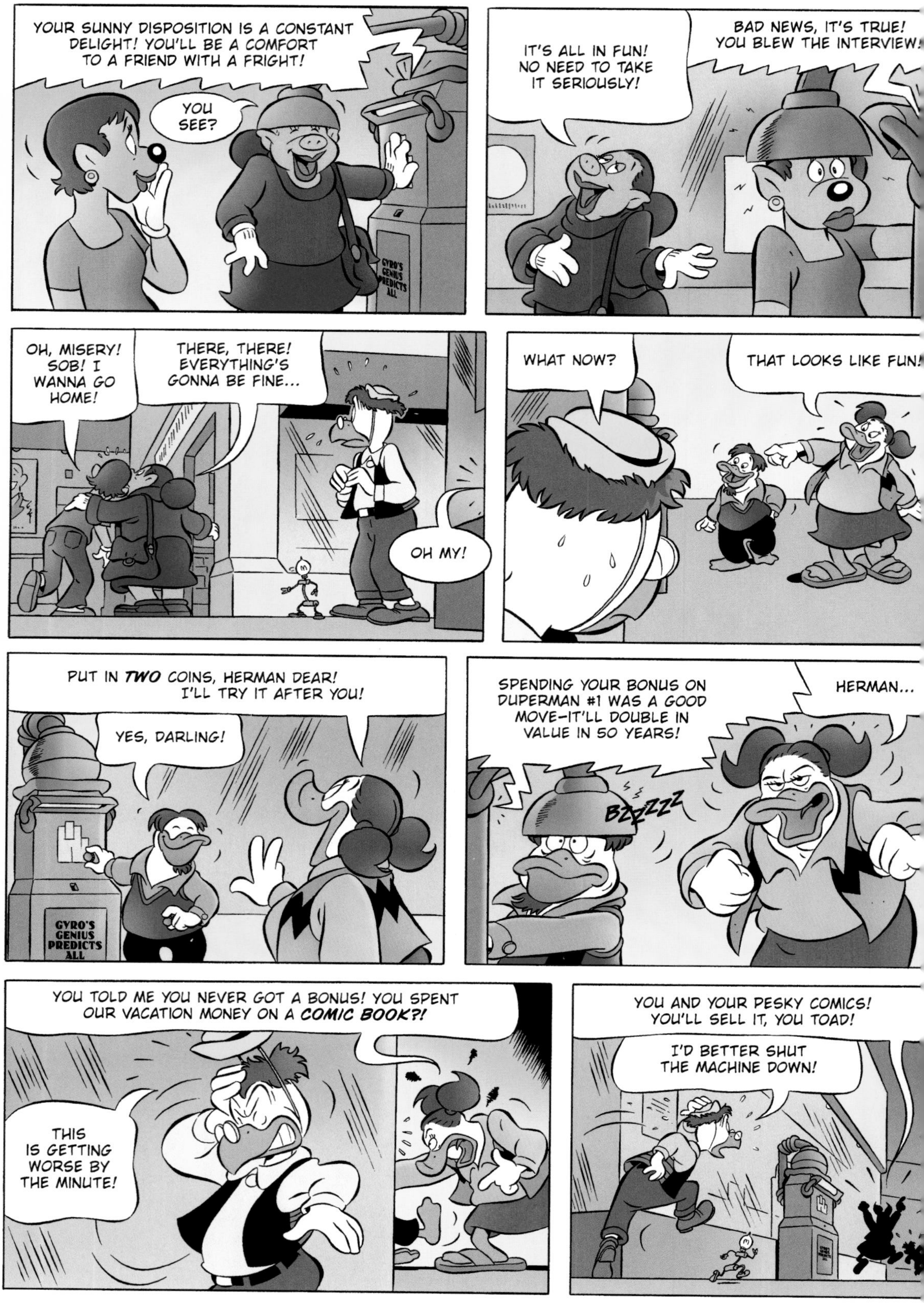
YOUR SUNNY DISPOSITION IS A CONSTANT DELIGHT! YOU'LL BE A COMFORT TO A FRIEND WITH A FRIGHT!
YOU SEE?
GYRO'S GENIUS PREDICTS ALL
IT'S ALL IN FUN! NO NEED TO TAKE IT SERIOUSLY!
BAD NEWS, IT'S TRUE! YOU BLEW THE INTERVIEW!
OH, MISERY! SOB! I WANNA GO HOME!
THERE, THERE! EVERYTHING'S GONNA BE FINE...
OH MY!
WHAT NOW?
THAT LOOKS LIKE FUN!
PUT IN TWO COINS, HERMAN DEAR! I'LL TRY IT AFTER YOU!
YES, DARLING!
GYRO'S GENIUS PREDICTS ALL
SPENDING YOUR BONUS ON DUPERMAN #1 WAS A GOOD MOVE–IT'LL DOUBLE IN VALUE IN 50 YEARS!
BZZZZZ
HERMAN...
YOU TOLD ME YOU NEVER GOT A BONUS! YOU SPENT OUR VACATION MONEY ON A COMIC BOOK?!
THIS IS GETTING WORSE BY THE MINUTE!
YOU AND YOUR PESKY COMICS! YOU'LL SELL IT, YOU TOAD!
I'D BETTER SHUT THE MACHINE DOWN!

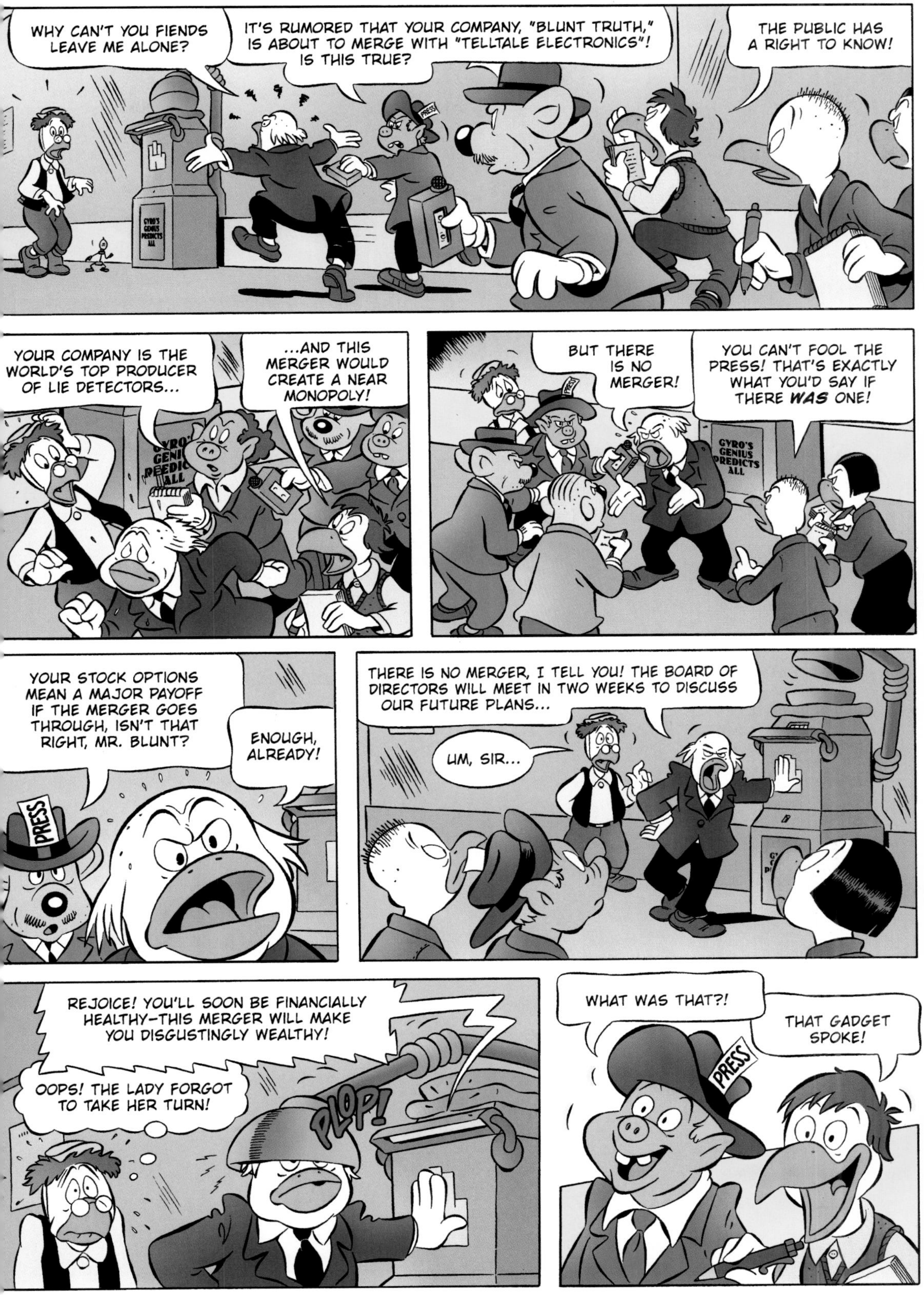
WHY CAN'T YOU FIENDS LEAVE ME ALONE?
IT'S RUMORED THAT YOUR COMPANY, "BLUNT TRUTH," IS ABOUT TO MERGE WITH "TELLTALE ELECTRONICS"! IS THIS TRUE?
THE PUBLIC HAS A RIGHT TO KNOW!
GYRO'S GENIUS PREDICTS ALL
PRESS
YOUR COMPANY IS THE WORLD'S TOP PRODUCER OF LIE DETECTORS...
...AND THIS MERGER WOULD CREATE A NEAR MONOPOLY!
BUT THERE IS NO MERGER!
YOU CAN'T FOOL THE PRESS! THAT'S EXACTLY WHAT YOU'D SAY IF THERE WAS ONE!
GYRO'S GENIUS PREDICTS ALL
YOUR STOCK OPTIONS MEAN A MAJOR PAYOFF IF THE MERGER GOES THROUGH, ISN'T THAT RIGHT, MR. BLUNT?
ENOUGH, ALREADY!
PRESS
THERE IS NO MERGER, I TELL YOU! THE BOARD OF DIRECTORS WILL MEET IN TWO WEEKS TO DISCUSS OUR FUTURE PLANS...
UM, SIR...
REJOICE! YOU'LL SOON BE FINANCIALLY HEALTHY—THIS MERGER WILL MAKE YOU DISGUSTINGLY WEALTHY!
OOPS! THE LADY FORGOT TO TAKE HER TURN!
PLOP!
WHAT WAS THAT?!
THAT GADGET SPOKE!
PRESS

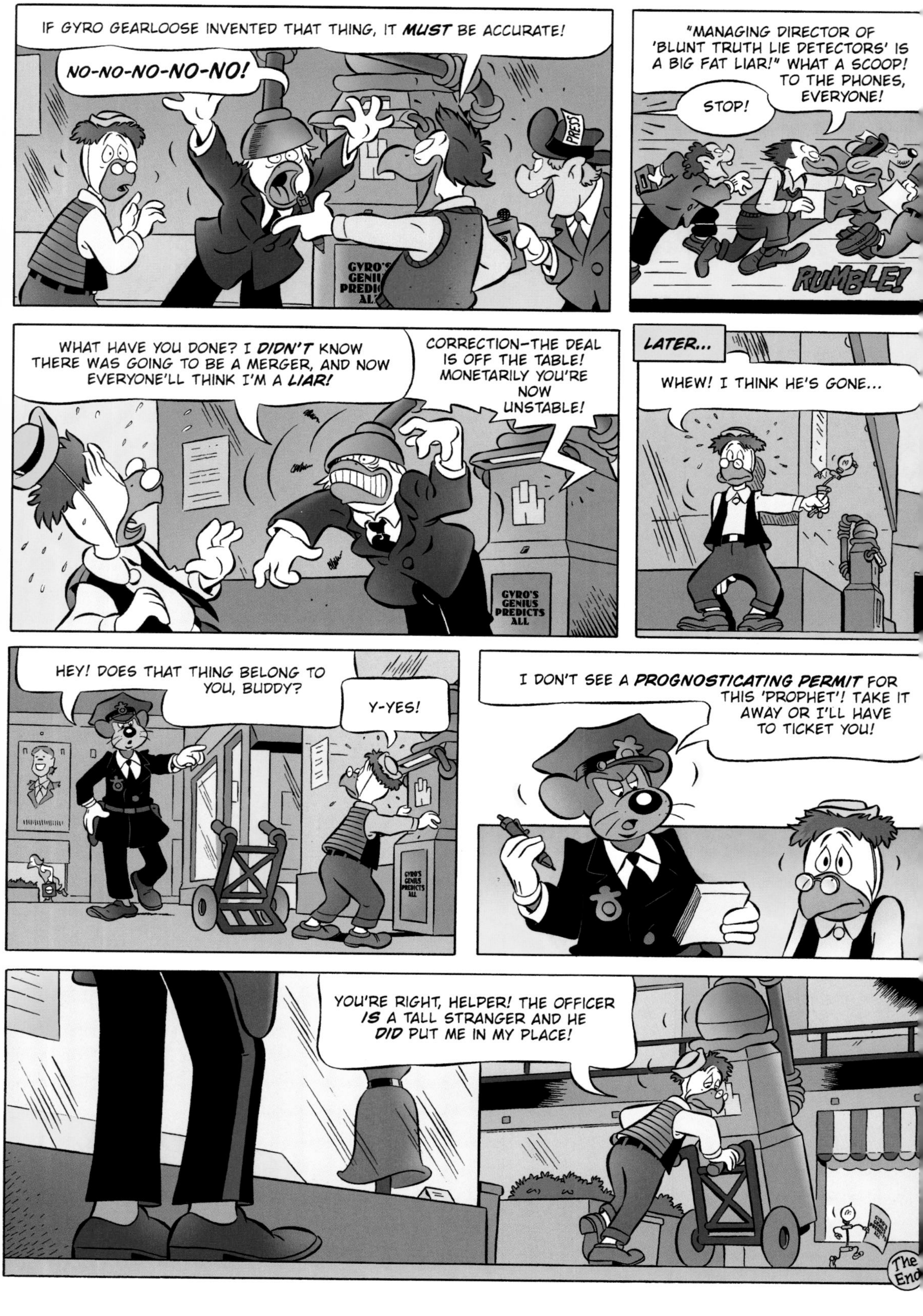

IF GYRO GEARLOOSE INVENTED THAT THING, IT MUST BE ACCURATE!
NO-NO-NO-NO-NO!
PRESS
GYRO'S GENIUS PREDIC ALL
"MANAGING DIRECTOR OF 'BLUNT TRUTH LIE DETECTORS' IS A BIG FAT LIAR!" WHAT A SCOOP! TO THE PHONES, EVERYONE!
STOP!
RUMBLE!
WHAT HAVE YOU DONE? I DIDN'T KNOW THERE WAS GOING TO BE A MERGER, AND NOW EVERYONE'LL THINK I'M A LIAR!
CORRECTION—THE DEAL IS OFF THE TABLE! MONETARILY YOU'RE NOW UNSTABLE!
GYRO'S GENIUS PREDICTS ALL
LATER...
WHEW! I THINK HE'S GONE...
HEY! DOES THAT THING BELONG TO YOU, BUDDY?
Y-YES!
I DON'T SEE A PROGNOSTICATING PERMIT FOR THIS 'PROPHET'! TAKE IT AWAY OR I'LL HAVE TO TICKET YOU!
YOU'RE RIGHT, HELPER! THE OFFICER IS A TALL STRANGER AND HE DID PUT ME IN MY PLACE!
The End

Walt Disney's Grandma Duck in Grandma vs. Grandma

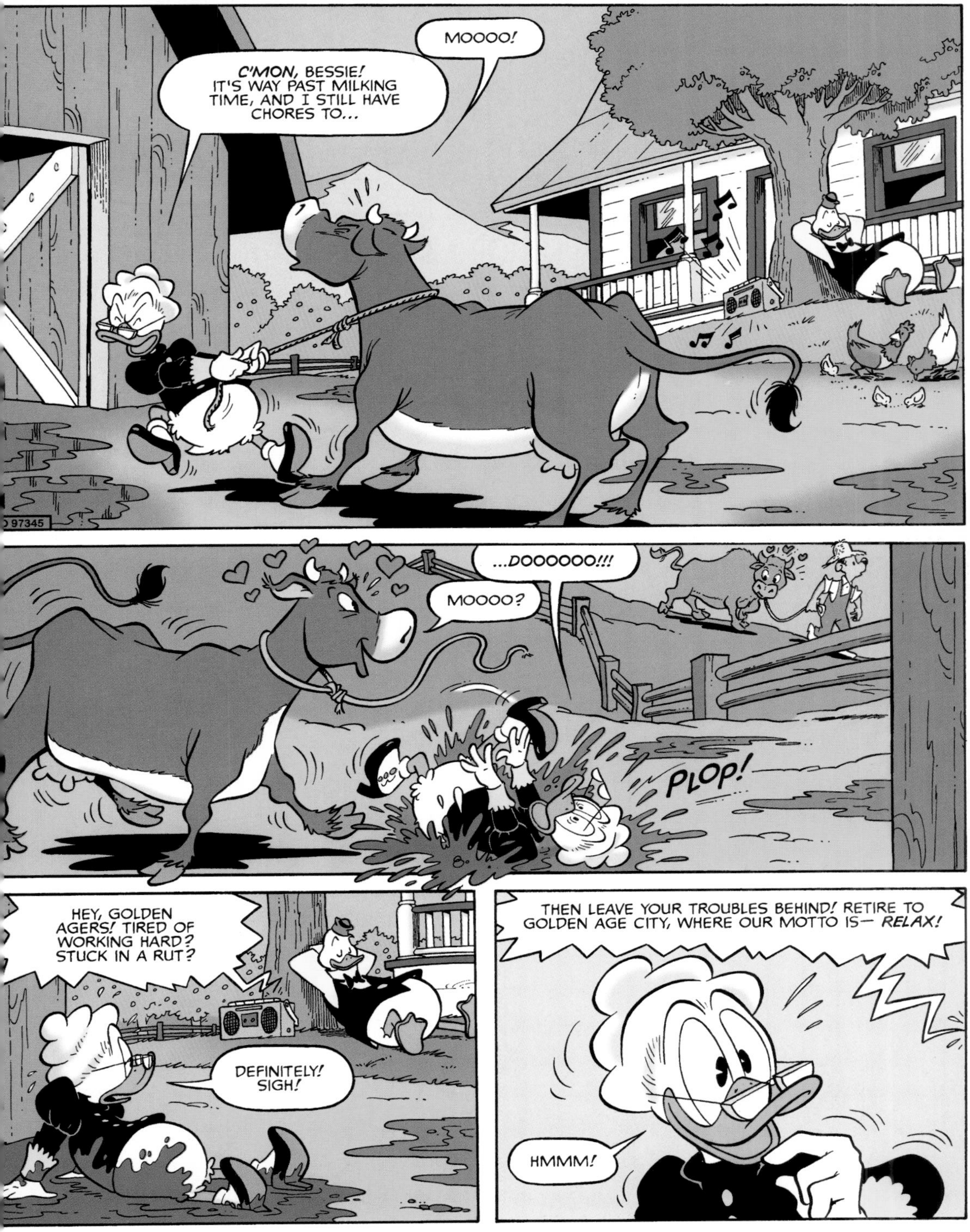
C'MON, BESSIE! IT'S WAY PAST MILKING TIME, AND I STILL HAVE CHORES TO...
MOOOO!
D 97345
MOOOO?
...DOOOOOO!!!
PLOP!
HEY, GOLDEN AGERS! TIRED OF WORKING HARD? STUCK IN A RUT?
DEFINITELY! SIGH!
THEN LEAVE YOUR TROUBLES BEHIND! RETIRE TO GOLDEN AGE CITY, WHERE OUR MOTTO IS— RELAX!
HMMM!

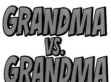

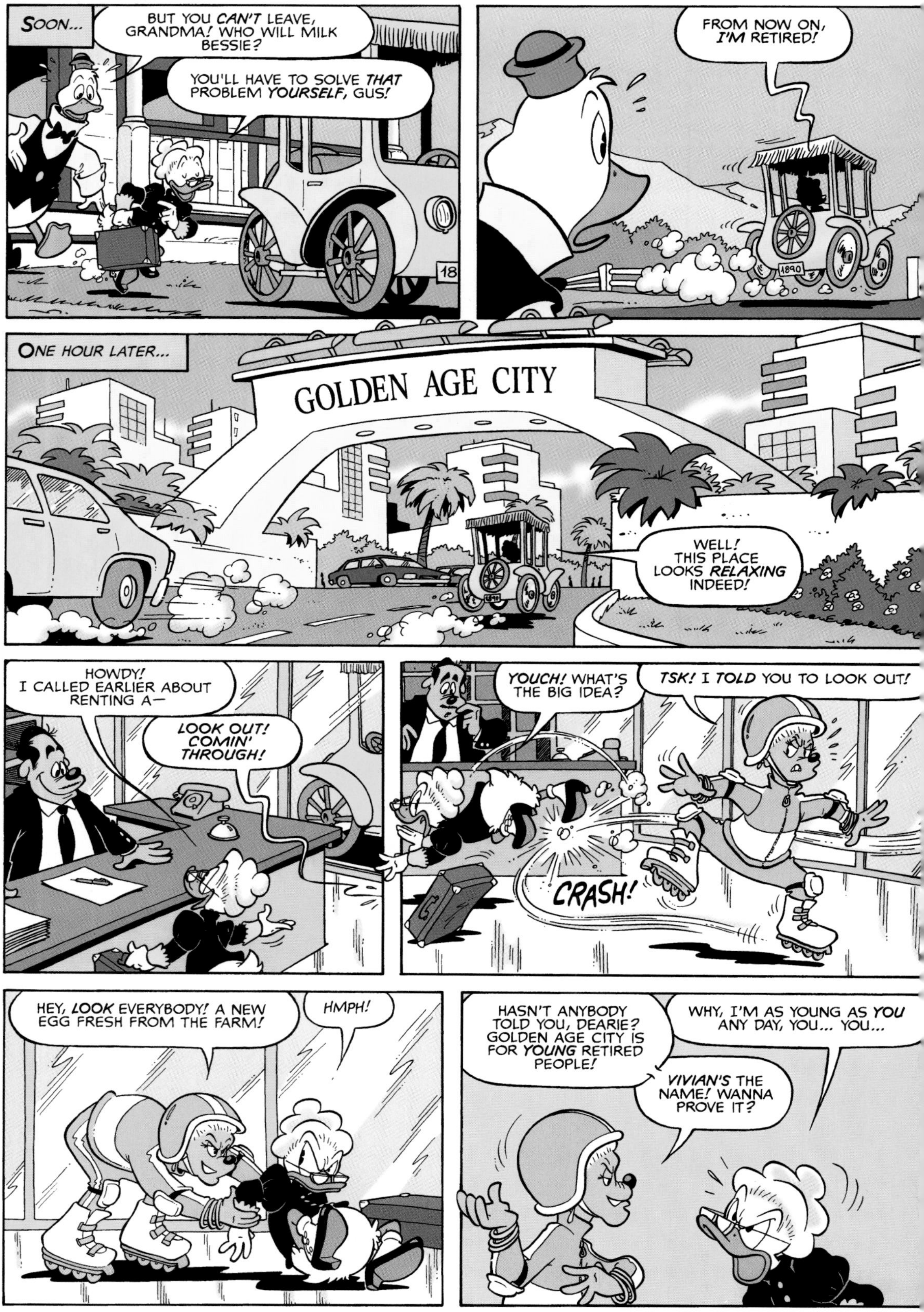
SOON...
BUT YOU *CAN'T* LEAVE, GRANDMA! WHO WILL MILK BESSIE?
YOU'LL HAVE TO SOLVE *THAT* PROBLEM *YOURSELF*, GUS!
FROM NOW ON, *I'M* RETIRED!
1890
ONE HOUR LATER...
GOLDEN AGE CITY
WELL! THIS PLACE LOOKS *RELAXING* INDEED!
HOWDY! I CALLED EARLIER ABOUT RENTING A—
LOOK OUT! COMIN' THROUGH!
YOUCH! WHAT'S THE BIG IDEA?
TSK! I *TOLD* YOU TO LOOK OUT!
CRASH!
HEY, *LOOK* EVERYBODY! A NEW EGG FRESH FROM THE FARM!
HMPH!
HASN'T ANYBODY TOLD YOU, DEARIE? GOLDEN AGE CITY IS FOR *YOUNG* RETIRED PEOPLE!
WHY, I'M AS YOUNG AS *YOU* ANY DAY, YOU... YOU...
VIVIAN'S THE NAME! WANNA PROVE IT?

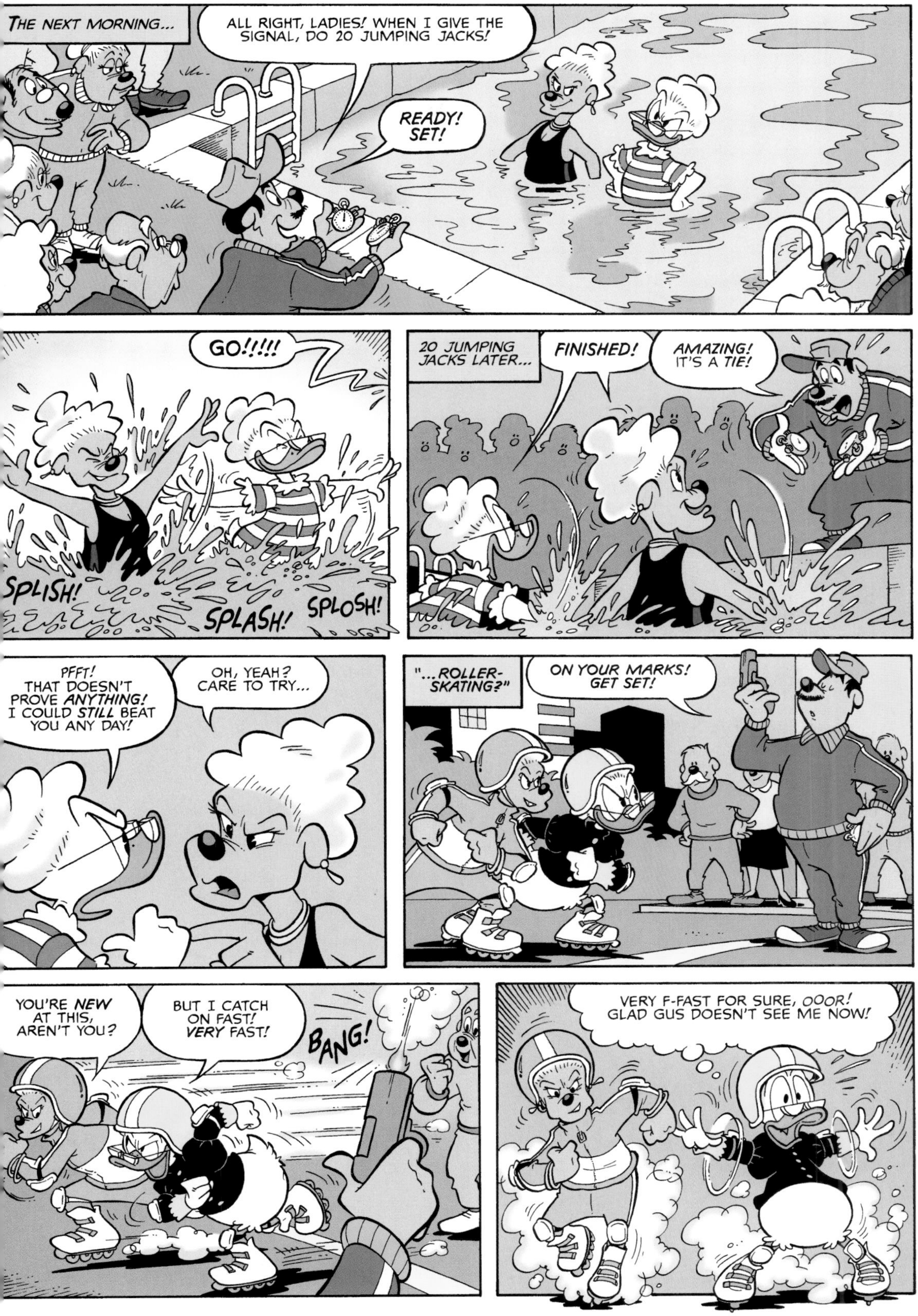
THE NEXT MORNING...
ALL RIGHT, LADIES! WHEN I GIVE THE SIGNAL, DO 20 JUMPING JACKS!
READY! SET!
GO!!!!!
SPLISH!
SPLASH!
SPLOSH!
20 JUMPING JACKS LATER...
FINISHED!
AMAZING! IT'S A TIE!
PFFT! THAT DOESN'T PROVE ANYTHING! I COULD STILL BEAT YOU ANY DAY!
OH, YEAH? CARE TO TRY...
"...ROLLER-SKATING?"
ON YOUR MARKS! GET SET!
YOU'RE NEW AT THIS, AREN'T YOU?
BUT I CATCH ON FAST! VERY FAST!
BANG!
VERY F-FAST FOR SURE, OOOR! GLAD GUS DOESN'T SEE ME NOW!

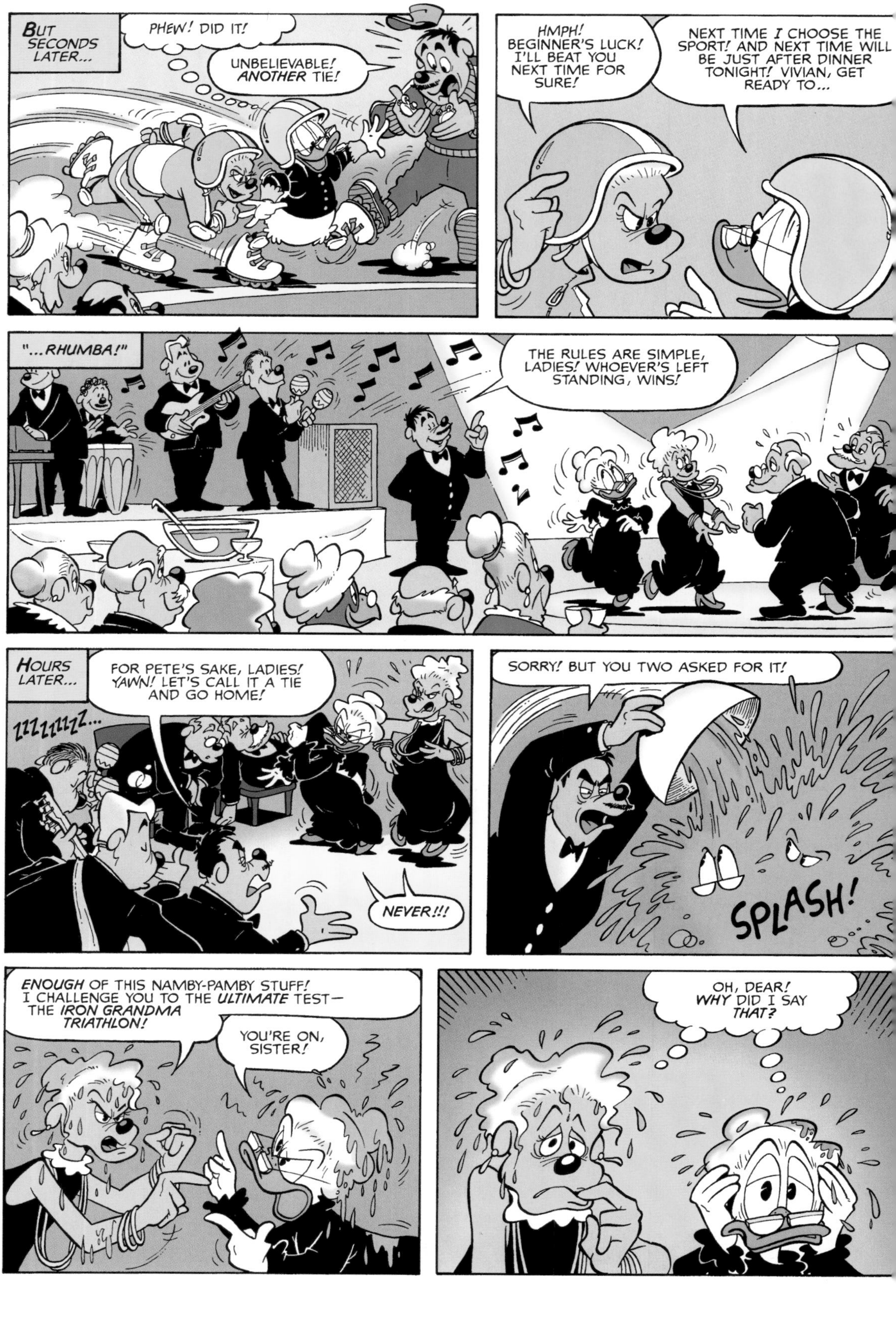
BUT SECONDS LATER...
PHEW! DID IT!
UNBELIEVABLE! ANOTHER TIE!
HMPH! BEGINNER'S LUCK! I'LL BEAT YOU NEXT TIME FOR SURE!
NEXT TIME I CHOOSE THE SPORT! AND NEXT TIME WILL BE JUST AFTER DINNER TONIGHT! VIVIAN, GET READY TO...
"...RHUMBA!"
THE RULES ARE SIMPLE, LADIES! WHOEVER'S LEFT STANDING, WINS!
HOURS LATER...
FOR PETE'S SAKE, LADIES! YAWN! LET'S CALL IT A TIE AND GO HOME!
ZZZZZZZZ...
NEVER!!!
SORRY! BUT YOU TWO ASKED FOR IT!
SPLASH!
ENOUGH OF THIS NAMBY-PAMBY STUFF! I CHALLENGE YOU TO THE ULTIMATE TEST— THE IRON GRANDMA TRIATHLON!
YOU'RE ON, SISTER!
OH, DEAR! WHY DID I SAY THAT?

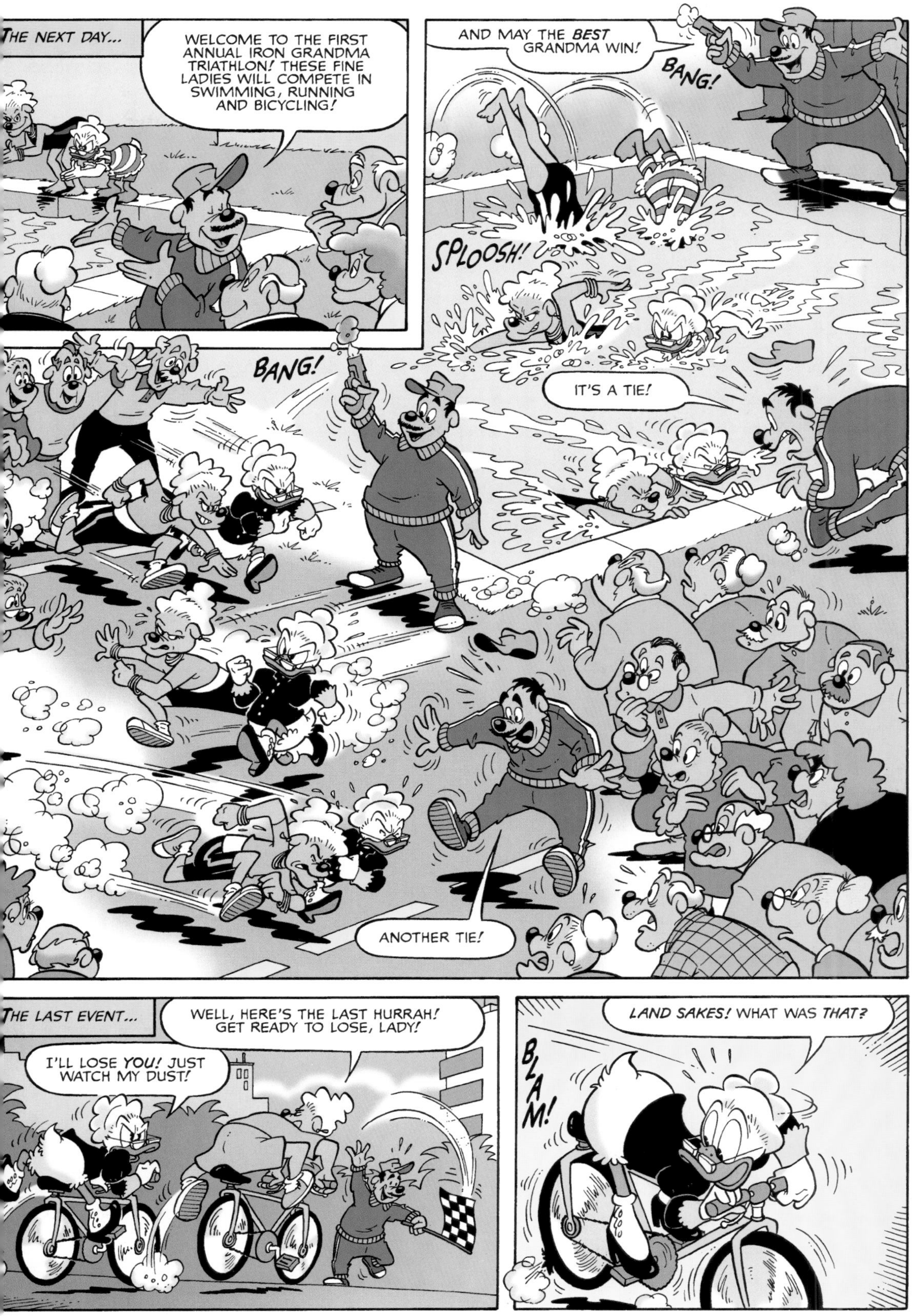

THE NEXT DAY...
WELCOME TO THE FIRST ANNUAL IRON GRANDMA TRIATHLON! THESE FINE LADIES WILL COMPETE IN SWIMMING, RUNNING AND BICYCLING!
AND MAY THE BEST GRANDMA WIN!
BANG!
SPLOOSH!
IT'S A TIE!
BANG!
ANOTHER TIE!
THE LAST EVENT...
WELL, HERE'S THE LAST HURRAH! GET READY TO LOSE, LADY!
I'LL LOSE YOU! JUST WATCH MY DUST!
LAND SAKES! WHAT WAS THAT?
BLAM!

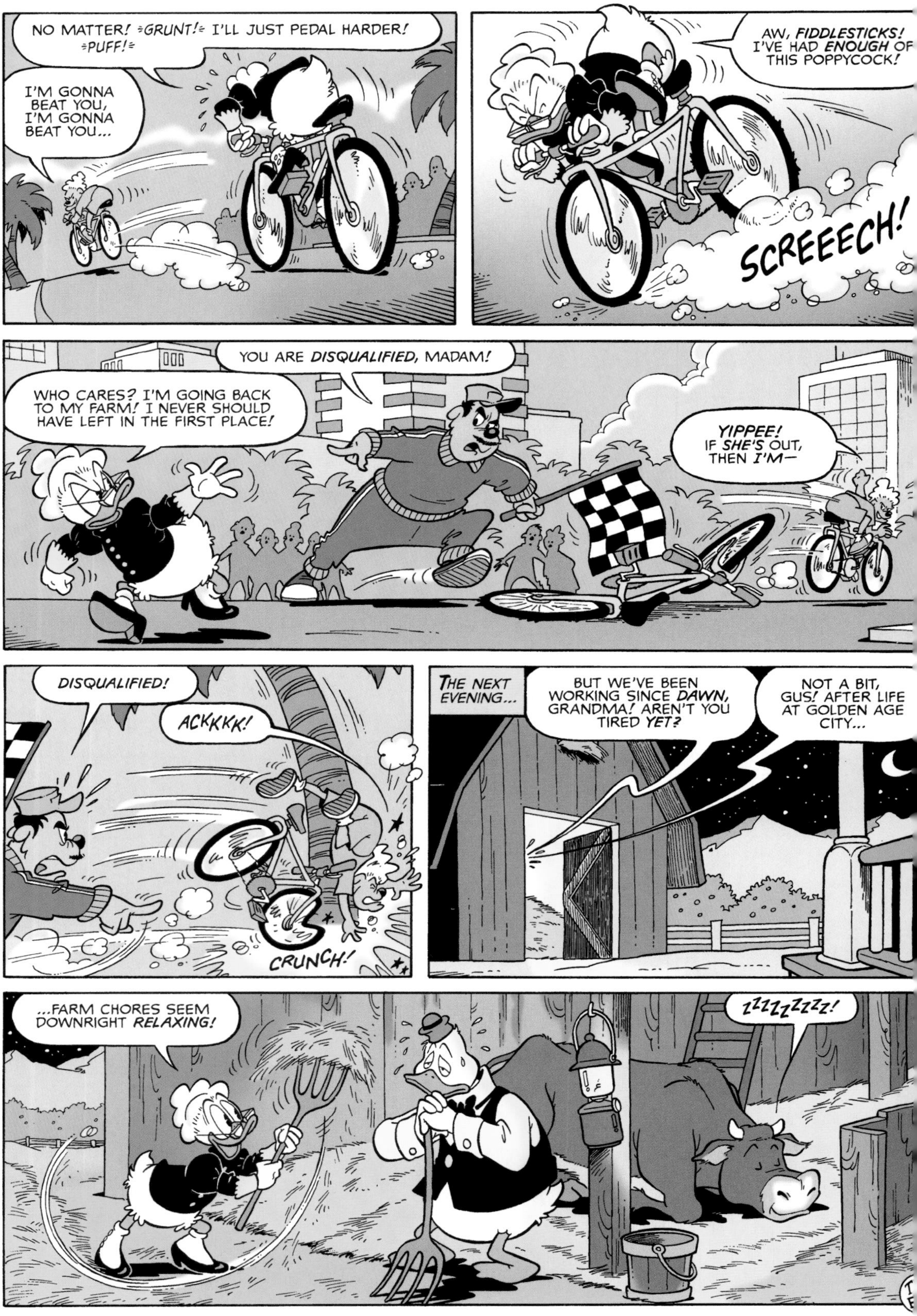
NO MATTER! =GRUNT!= I'LL JUST PEDAL HARDER! =PUFF!=
I'M GONNA BEAT YOU, I'M GONNA BEAT YOU...
AW, FIDDLESTICKS! I'VE HAD ENOUGH OF THIS POPPYCOCK!
SCREEECH!
YOU ARE DISQUALIFIED, MADAM!
WHO CARES? I'M GOING BACK TO MY FARM! I NEVER SHOULD HAVE LEFT IN THE FIRST PLACE!
YIPPEE! IF SHE'S OUT, THEN I'M—
DISQUALIFIED!
ACKKKK!
CRUNCH!
THE NEXT EVENING...
BUT WE'VE BEEN WORKING SINCE DAWN, GRANDMA! AREN'T YOU TIRED YET?
NOT A BIT, GUS! AFTER LIFE AT GOLDEN AGE CITY...
...FARM CHORES SEEM DOWNRIGHT RELAXING!
ZZZZZZZZZZ!

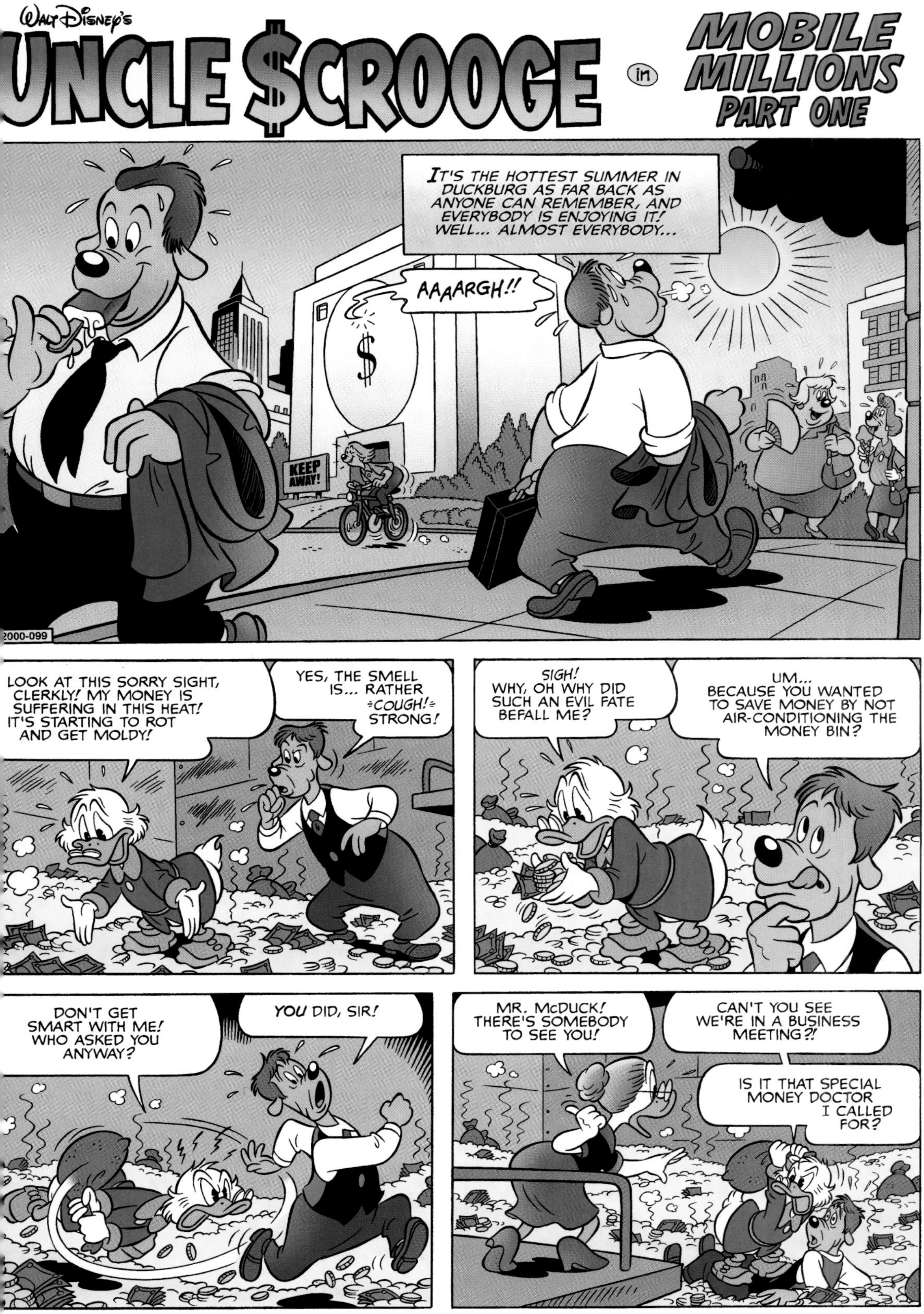
Walt Disney's
UNCLE $CROOGE
in
MOBILE MILLIONS
PART ONE
IT'S THE HOTTEST SUMMER IN DUCKBURG AS FAR BACK AS ANYONE CAN REMEMBER, AND EVERYBODY IS ENJOYING IT! WELL... ALMOST EVERYBODY...
AAAARGH!!
KEEP AWAY!
2000-099
LOOK AT THIS SORRY SIGHT, CLERKLY! MY MONEY IS SUFFERING IN THIS HEAT! IT'S STARTING TO ROT AND GET MOLDY!
YES, THE SMELL IS... RATHER =COUGH!= STRONG!
SIGH! WHY, OH WHY DID SUCH AN EVIL FATE BEFALL ME?
UM... BECAUSE YOU WANTED TO SAVE MONEY BY NOT AIR-CONDITIONING THE MONEY BIN?
DON'T GET SMART WITH ME! WHO ASKED YOU ANYWAY?
YOU DID, SIR!
MR. McDUCK! THERE'S SOMEBODY TO SEE YOU!
CAN'T YOU SEE WE'RE IN A BUSINESS MEETING?!
IS IT THAT SPECIAL MONEY DOCTOR I CALLED FOR?

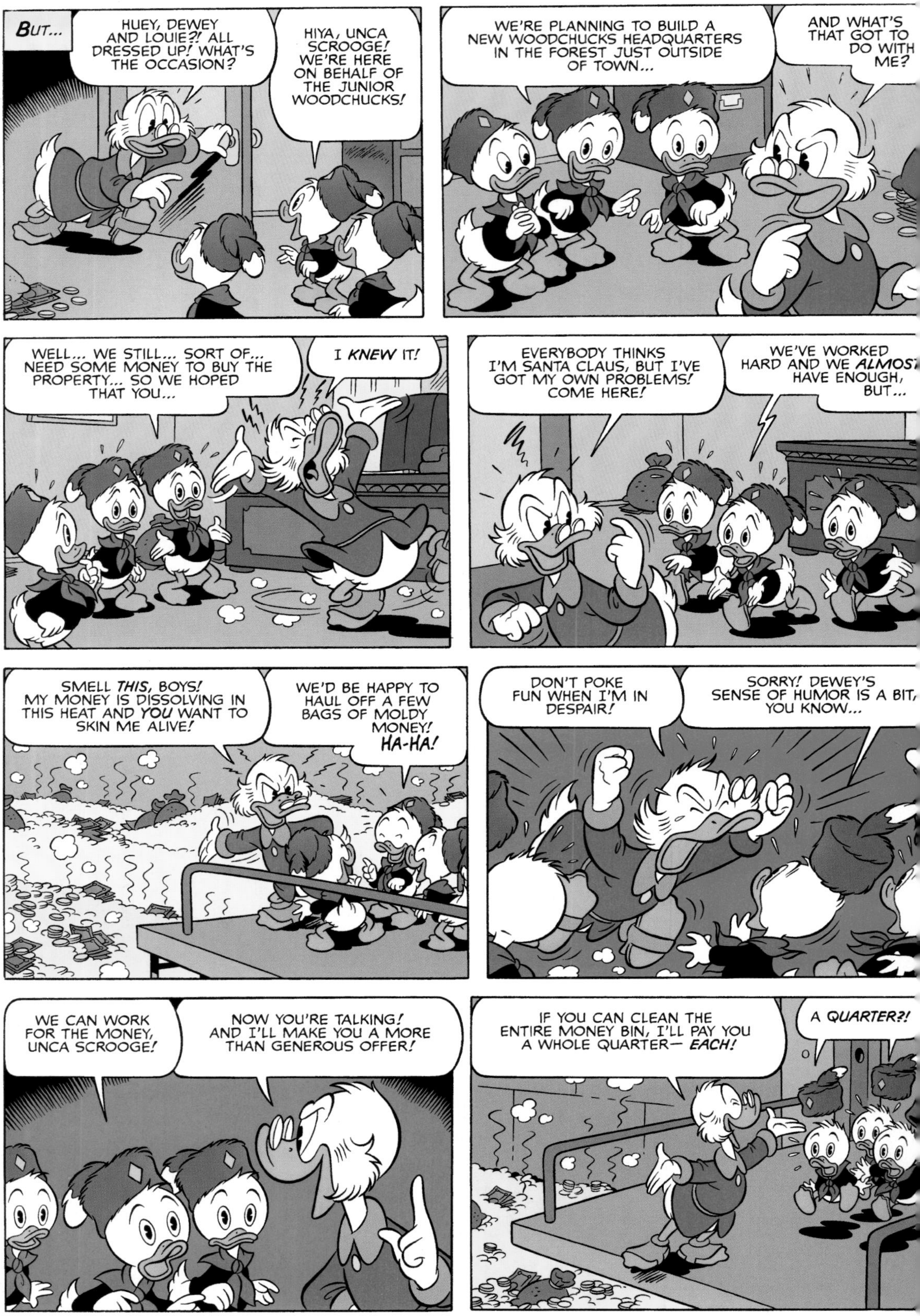

BUT...
HUEY, DEWEY AND LOUIE?! ALL DRESSED UP! WHAT'S THE OCCASION?
HIYA, UNCA SCROOGE! WE'RE HERE ON BEHALF OF THE JUNIOR WOODCHUCKS!
WE'RE PLANNING TO BUILD A NEW WOODCHUCKS HEADQUARTERS IN THE FOREST JUST OUTSIDE OF TOWN...
AND WHAT'S THAT GOT TO DO WITH ME?
WELL... WE STILL... SORT OF... NEED SOME MONEY TO BUY THE PROPERTY... SO WE HOPED THAT YOU...
I KNEW IT!
EVERYBODY THINKS I'M SANTA CLAUS, BUT I'VE GOT MY OWN PROBLEMS! COME HERE!
WE'VE WORKED HARD AND WE ALMOS HAVE ENOUGH, BUT...
SMELL THIS, BOYS! MY MONEY IS DISSOLVING IN THIS HEAT AND YOU WANT TO SKIN ME ALIVE!
WE'D BE HAPPY TO HAUL OFF A FEW BAGS OF MOLDY MONEY! HA-HA!
DON'T POKE FUN WHEN I'M IN DESPAIR!
SORRY! DEWEY'S SENSE OF HUMOR IS A BIT, YOU KNOW...
WE CAN WORK FOR THE MONEY, UNCA SCROOGE!
NOW YOU'RE TALKING! AND I'LL MAKE YOU A MORE THAN GENEROUS OFFER!
IF YOU CAN CLEAN THE ENTIRE MONEY BIN, I'LL PAY YOU A WHOLE QUARTER— EACH!
A QUARTER?!

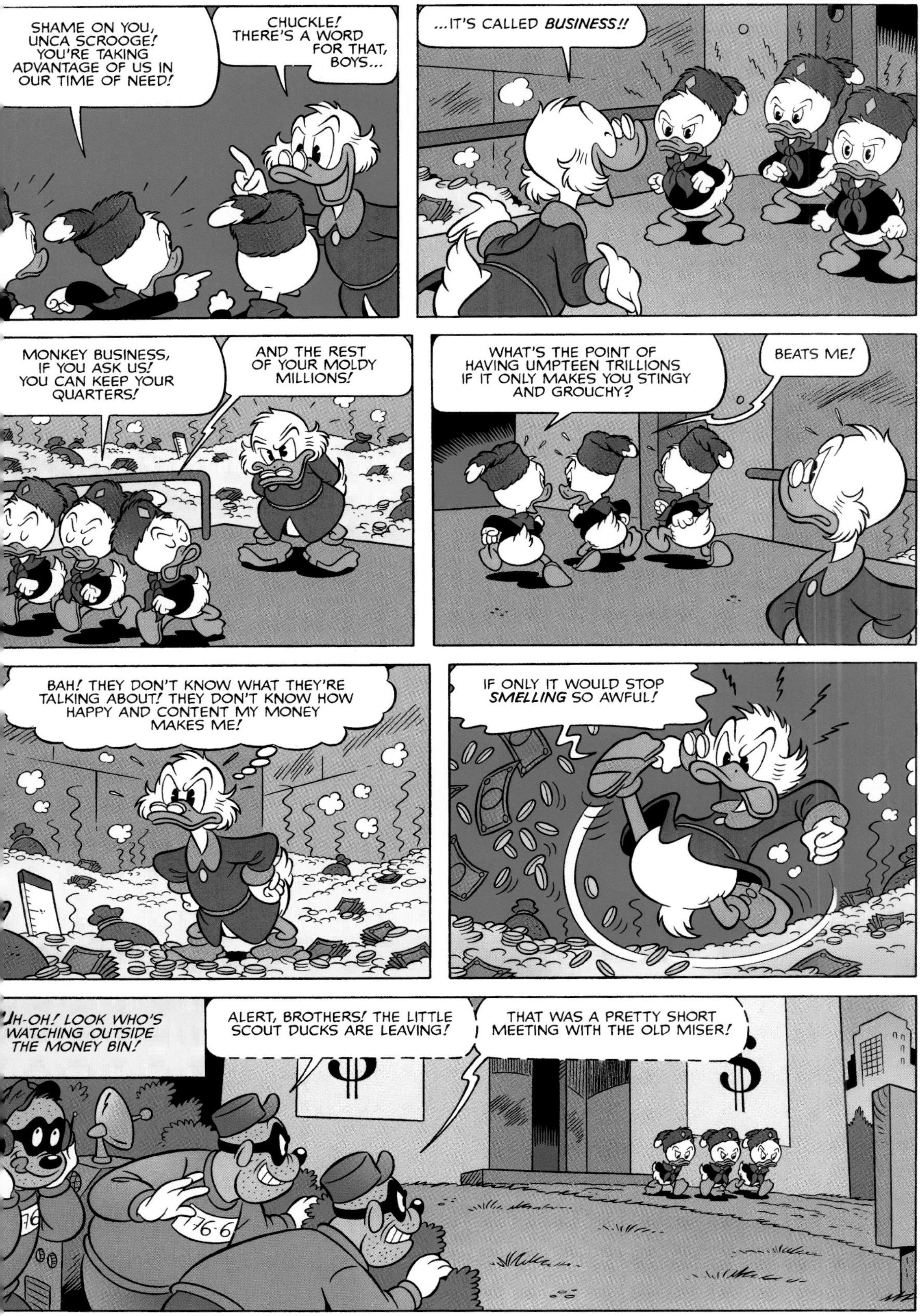
SHAME ON YOU, UNCA SCROOGE! YOU'RE TAKING ADVANTAGE OF US IN OUR TIME OF NEED!
CHUCKLE! THERE'S A WORD FOR THAT, BOYS...
...IT'S CALLED BUSINESS!!
MONKEY BUSINESS, IF YOU ASK US! YOU CAN KEEP YOUR QUARTERS!
AND THE REST OF YOUR MOLDY MILLIONS!
WHAT'S THE POINT OF HAVING UMPTEEN TRILLIONS IF IT ONLY MAKES YOU STINGY AND GROUCHY?
BEATS ME!
BAH! THEY DON'T KNOW WHAT THEY'RE TALKING ABOUT! THEY DON'T KNOW HOW HAPPY AND CONTENT MY MONEY MAKES ME!
IF ONLY IT WOULD STOP SMELLING SO AWFUL!
UH-OH! LOOK WHO'S WATCHING OUTSIDE THE MONEY BIN!
ALERT, BROTHERS! THE LITTLE SCOUT DUCKS ARE LEAVING!
THAT WAS A PRETTY SHORT MEETING WITH THE OLD MISER!
176-6

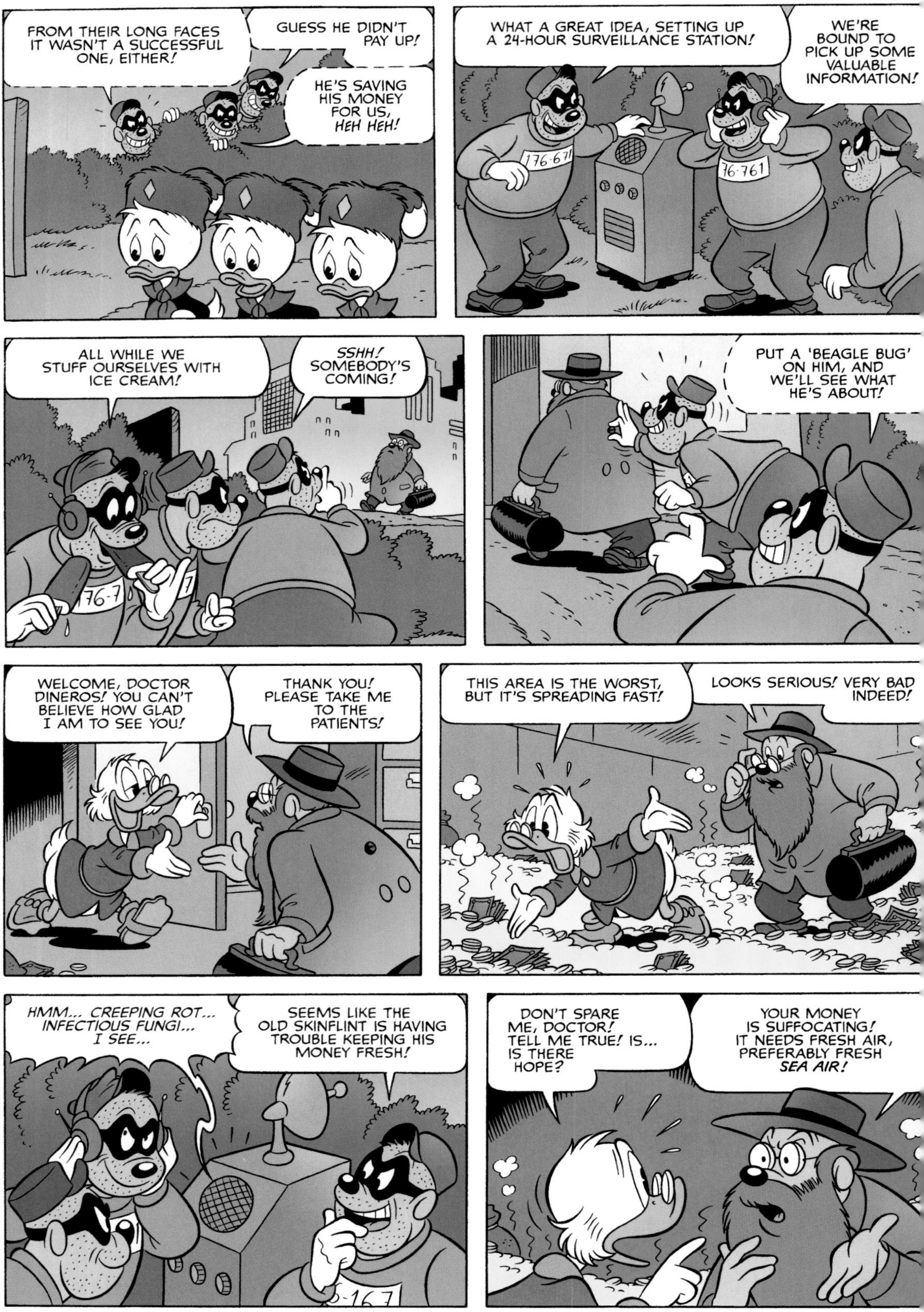
FROM THEIR LONG FACES IT WASN'T A SUCCESSFUL ONE, EITHER!
GUESS HE DIDN'T PAY UP!
HE'S SAVING HIS MONEY FOR US, *HEH HEH!*
WHAT A GREAT IDEA, SETTING UP A 24-HOUR SURVEILLANCE STATION!
WE'RE BOUND TO PICK UP SOME VALUABLE INFORMATION!
176-671
76-761
ALL WHILE WE STUFF OURSELVES WITH ICE CREAM!
SSHH! SOMEBODY'S COMING!
PUT A 'BEAGLE BUG' ON HIM, AND WE'LL SEE WHAT HE'S ABOUT!
WELCOME, DOCTOR DINEROS! YOU CAN'T BELIEVE HOW GLAD I AM TO SEE YOU!
THANK YOU! PLEASE TAKE ME TO THE PATIENTS!
THIS AREA IS THE WORST, BUT IT'S SPREADING FAST!
LOOKS SERIOUS! VERY BAD INDEED!
HMM... CREEPING ROT... INFECTIOUS FUNGI... I SEE...
SEEMS LIKE THE OLD SKINFLINT IS HAVING TROUBLE KEEPING HIS MONEY FRESH!
DON'T SPARE ME, DOCTOR! TELL ME TRUE! IS... IS THERE HOPE?
YOUR MONEY IS SUFFOCATING! IT NEEDS FRESH AIR, PREFERABLY FRESH *SEA AIR!*

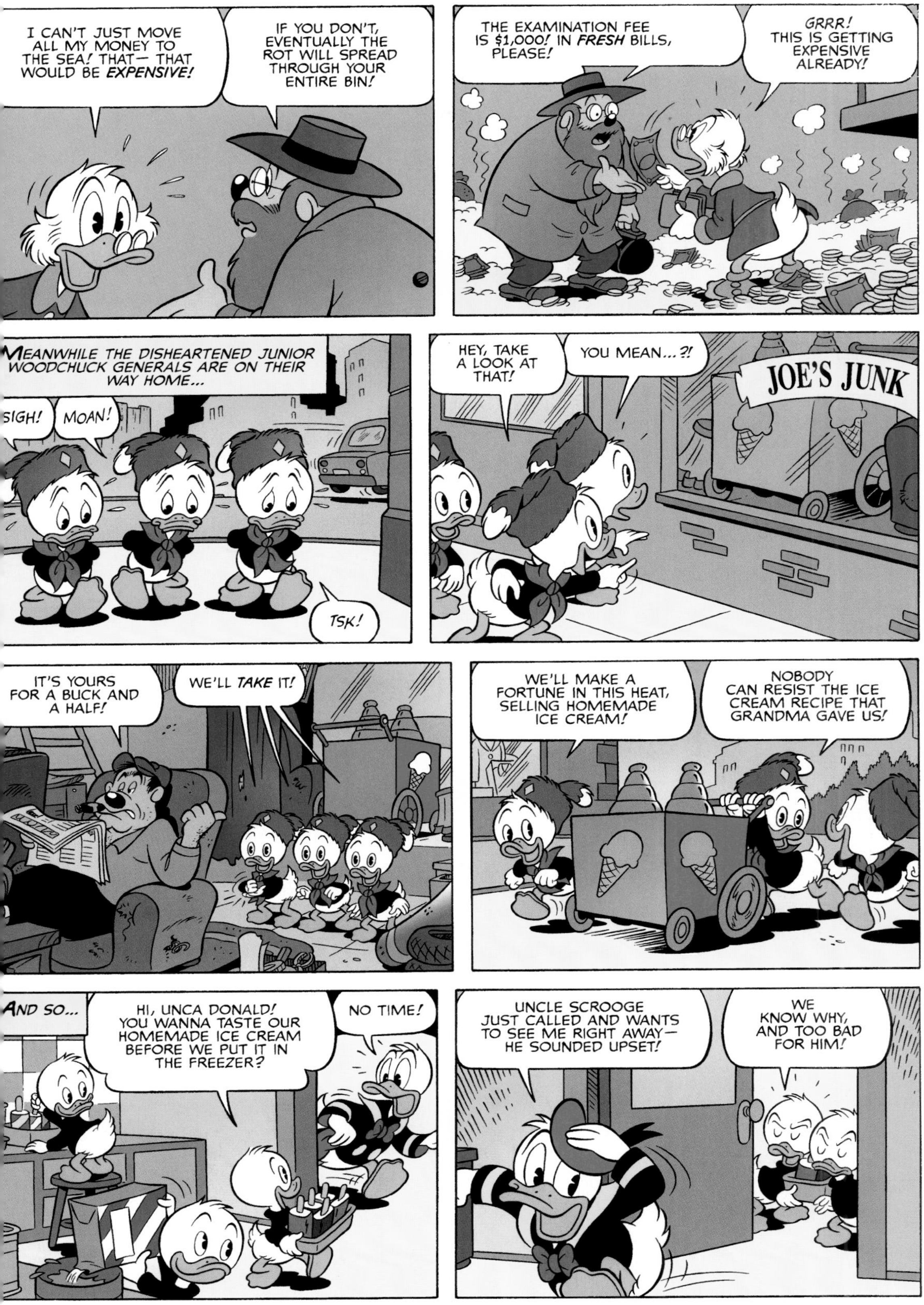
I CAN'T JUST MOVE ALL MY MONEY TO THE SEA! THAT— THAT WOULD BE EXPENSIVE!
IF YOU DON'T, EVENTUALLY THE ROT WILL SPREAD THROUGH YOUR ENTIRE BIN!
THE EXAMINATION FEE IS $1,000! IN FRESH BILLS, PLEASE!
GRRR! THIS IS GETTING EXPENSIVE ALREADY!
MEANWHILE THE DISHEARTENED JUNIOR WOODCHUCK GENERALS ARE ON THEIR WAY HOME...
SIGH!
MOAN!
TSK!
HEY, TAKE A LOOK AT THAT!
YOU MEAN...?!
JOE'S JUNK
IT'S YOURS FOR A BUCK AND A HALF!
WE'LL TAKE IT!
WE'LL MAKE A FORTUNE IN THIS HEAT, SELLING HOMEMADE ICE CREAM!
NOBODY CAN RESIST THE ICE CREAM RECIPE THAT GRANDMA GAVE US!
AND SO...
HI, UNCA DONALD! YOU WANNA TASTE OUR HOMEMADE ICE CREAM BEFORE WE PUT IT IN THE FREEZER?
NO TIME!
UNCLE SCROOGE JUST CALLED AND WANTS TO SEE ME RIGHT AWAY— HE SOUNDED UPSET!
WE KNOW WHY, AND TOO BAD FOR HIM!

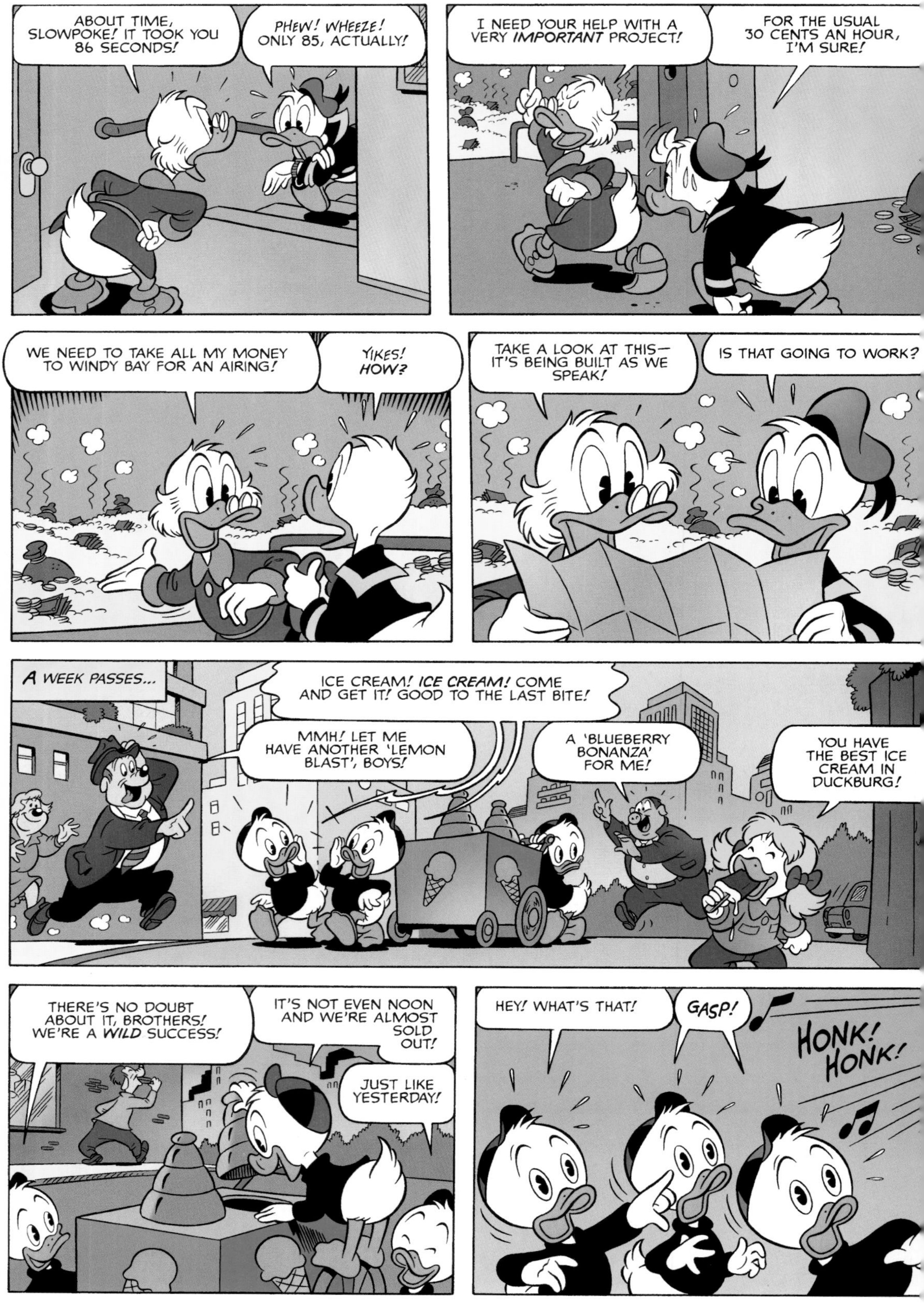
ABOUT TIME, SLOWPOKE! IT TOOK YOU 86 SECONDS!
PHEW! WHEEZE! ONLY 85, ACTUALLY!
I NEED YOUR HELP WITH A VERY IMPORTANT PROJECT!
FOR THE USUAL 30 CENTS AN HOUR, I'M SURE!
WE NEED TO TAKE ALL MY MONEY TO WINDY BAY FOR AN AIRING!
YIKES! HOW?
TAKE A LOOK AT THIS— IT'S BEING BUILT AS WE SPEAK!
IS THAT GOING TO WORK?
A WEEK PASSES...
ICE CREAM! ICE CREAM! COME AND GET IT! GOOD TO THE LAST BITE!
MMH! LET ME HAVE ANOTHER 'LEMON BLAST', BOYS!
A 'BLUEBERRY BONANZA' FOR ME!
YOU HAVE THE BEST ICE CREAM IN DUCKBURG!
THERE'S NO DOUBT ABOUT IT, BROTHERS! WE'RE A WILD SUCCESS!
IT'S NOT EVEN NOON AND WE'RE ALMOST SOLD OUT!
JUST LIKE YESTERDAY!
HEY! WHAT'S THAT!
GASP!
HONK! HONK!

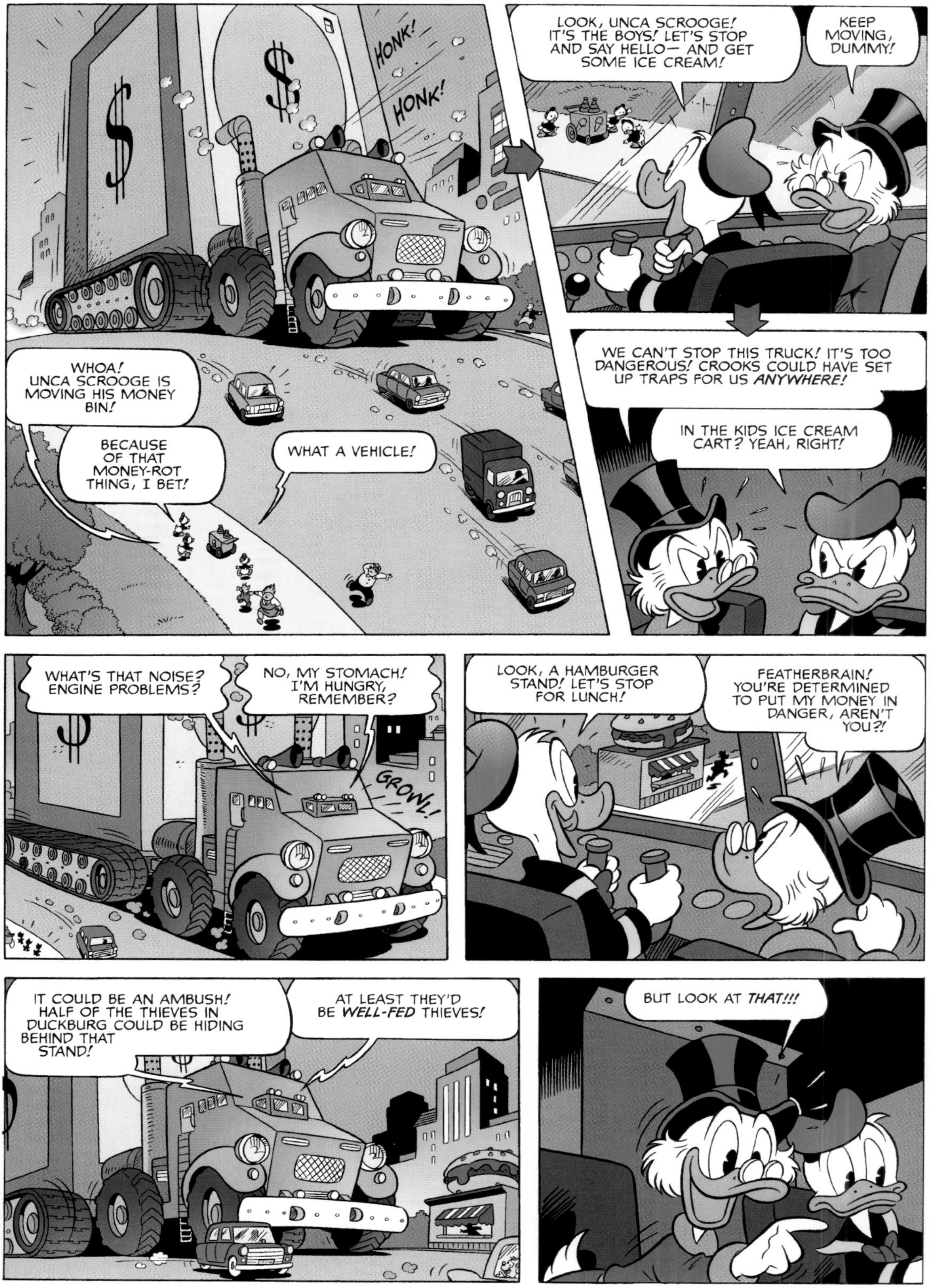
HONK!
HONK!
WHOA! UNCA SCROOGE IS MOVING HIS MONEY BIN!
BECAUSE OF THAT MONEY-ROT THING, I BET!
WHAT A VEHICLE!
LOOK, UNCA SCROOGE! IT'S THE BOYS! LET'S STOP AND SAY HELLO— AND GET SOME ICE CREAM!
KEEP MOVING, DUMMY!
WE CAN'T STOP THIS TRUCK! IT'S TOO DANGEROUS! CROOKS COULD HAVE SET UP TRAPS FOR US *ANYWHERE!*
IN THE KIDS ICE CREAM CART? YEAH, RIGHT!
WHAT'S THAT NOISE? ENGINE PROBLEMS?
NO, MY STOMACH! I'M HUNGRY, REMEMBER?
GROWL!
LOOK, A HAMBURGER STAND! LET'S STOP FOR LUNCH!
FEATHERBRAIN! YOU'RE DETERMINED TO PUT MY MONEY IN DANGER, AREN'T YOU?!
IT COULD BE AN AMBUSH! HALF OF THE THIEVES IN DUCKBURG COULD BE HIDING BEHIND THAT STAND!
AT LEAST THEY'D BE ***WELL-FED*** THIEVES!
BUT LOOK AT *THAT!!!*

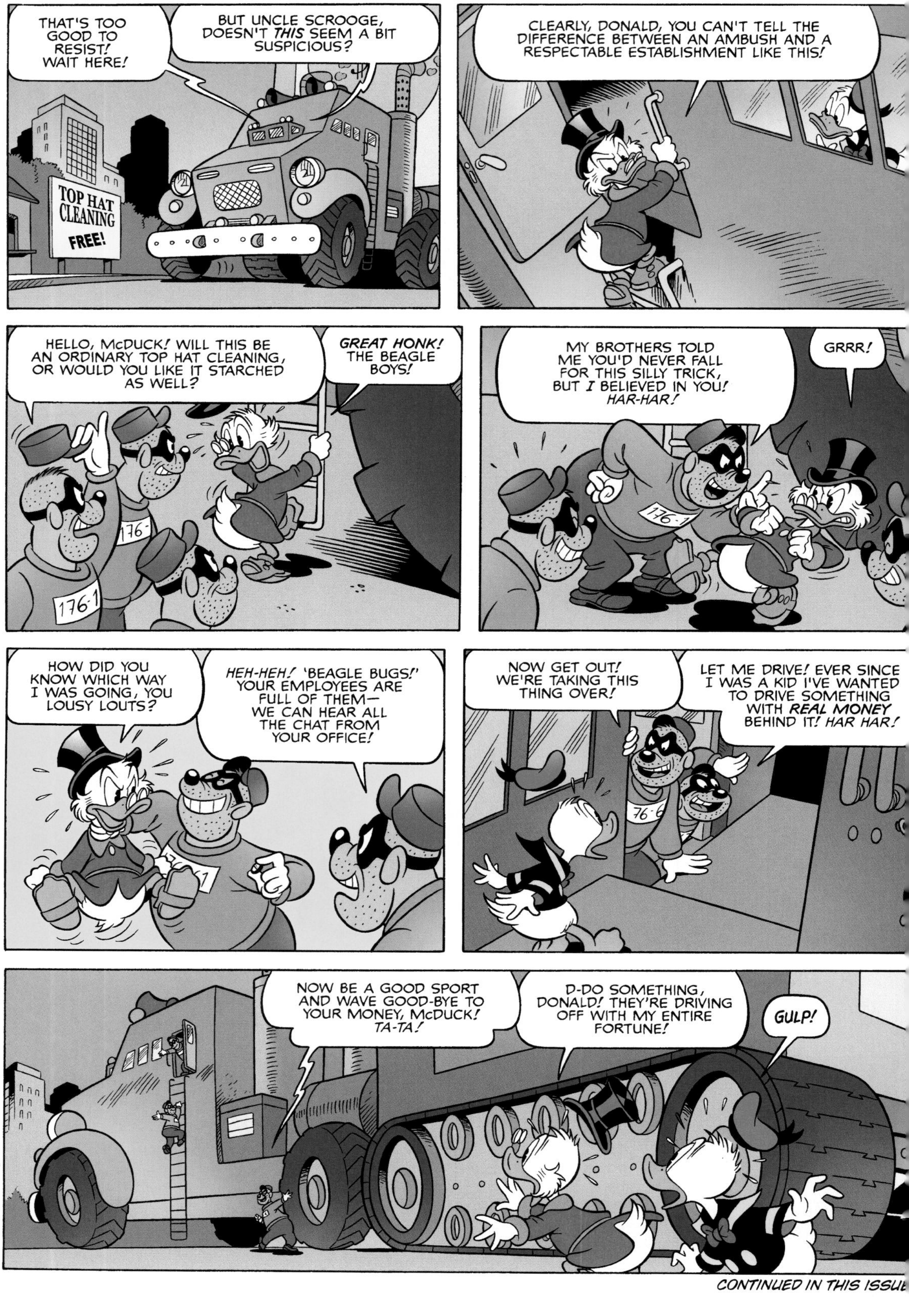
THAT'S TOO GOOD TO RESIST! WAIT HERE!
BUT UNCLE SCROOGE, DOESN'T *THIS* SEEM A BIT SUSPICIOUS?
TOP HAT CLEANING
FREE!
CLEARLY, DONALD, YOU CAN'T TELL THE DIFFERENCE BETWEEN AN AMBUSH AND A RESPECTABLE ESTABLISHMENT LIKE THIS!
HELLO, McDUCK! WILL THIS BE AN ORDINARY TOP HAT CLEANING, OR WOULD YOU LIKE IT STARCHED AS WELL?
GREAT HONK! THE BEAGLE BOYS!
176-1
MY BROTHERS TOLD ME YOU'D NEVER FALL FOR THIS SILLY TRICK, BUT *I* BELIEVED IN YOU! *HAR-HAR!*
GRRR!
HOW DID YOU KNOW WHICH WAY I WAS GOING, YOU LOUSY LOUTS?
HEH-HEH! 'BEAGLE BUGS!' YOUR EMPLOYEES ARE FULL OF THEM— WE CAN HEAR ALL THE CHAT FROM YOUR OFFICE!
NOW GET OUT! WE'RE TAKING THIS THING OVER!
LET ME DRIVE! EVER SINCE I WAS A KID I'VE WANTED TO DRIVE SOMETHING WITH *REAL MONEY* BEHIND IT! *HAR HAR!*
NOW BE A GOOD SPORT AND WAVE GOOD-BYE TO YOUR MONEY, McDUCK! *TA-TA!*
D-DO SOMETHING, DONALD! THEY'RE DRIVING OFF WITH MY ENTIRE FORTUNE!
GULP!

CONTINUED IN THIS ISSUE

Looking for a comics specialty store near you?

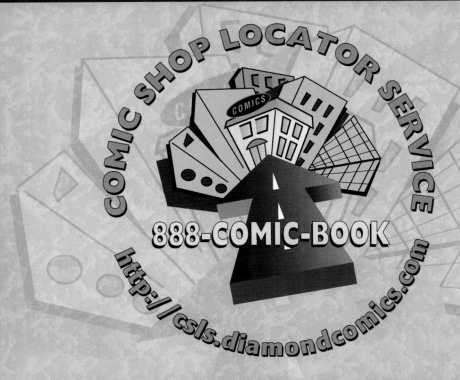

COMIC SHOP LOCATOR SERVICE

888-COMIC-BOOK

http://csls.diamondcomics.com

Use the service that has assisted millions of comic book fans worldwide—
the Comic Shop Locator Service!

By Phone: 1-888-COMIC-BOOK (toll-free!)
On the Internet: http://csls.diamondcomics.com

Fast. Fun. Free.

**Order from PREVIEWS,
the industry's preordering catalog!**

Pick up a copy at your local comics shop, or visit
PREVIEWS online at http://previews.diamondcomics.com
to see comics that will be in stores in two months!
Then go to your shop and place your order—
it doesn't get easier than that!

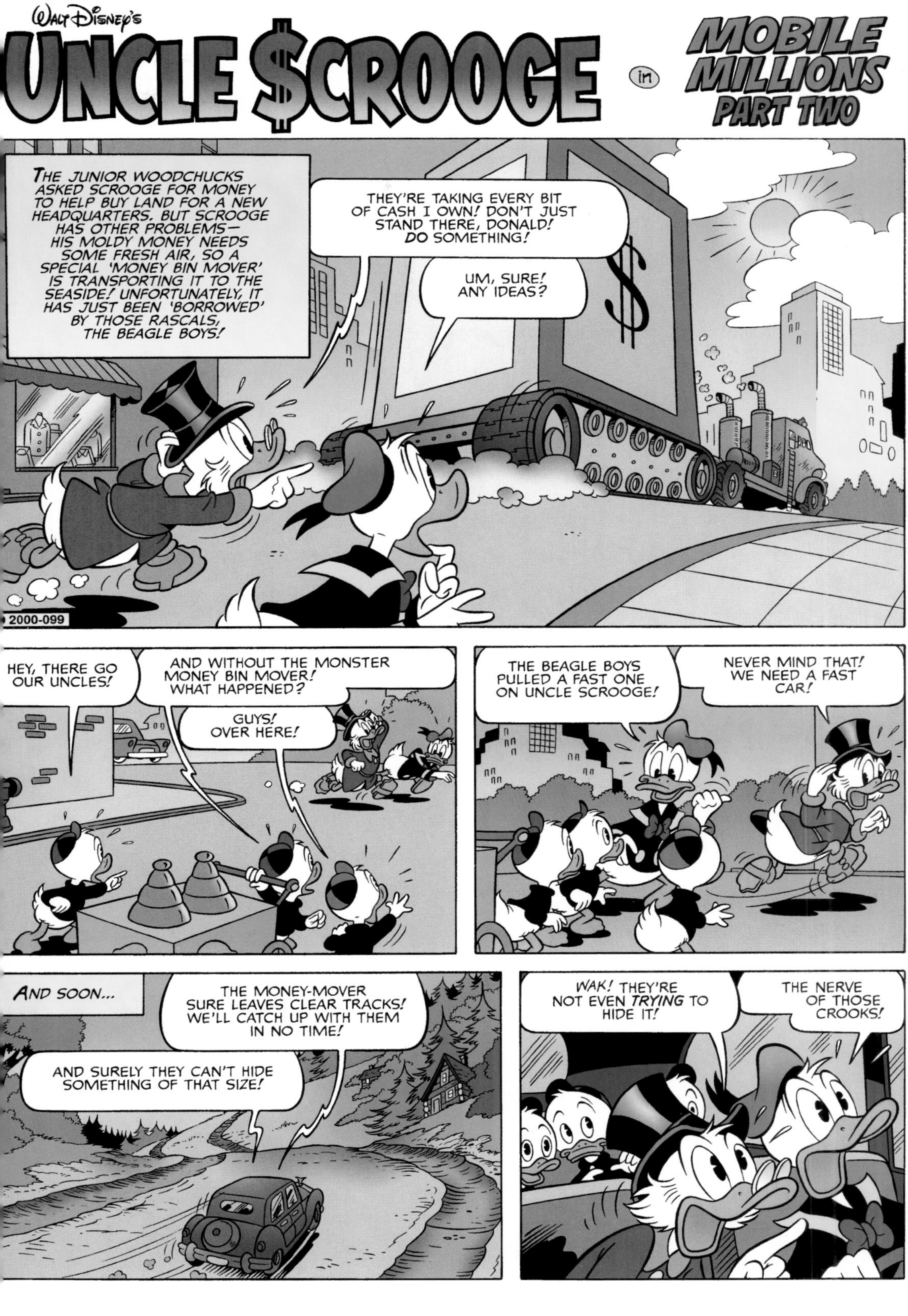
WALT DISNEY'S
UNCLE $CROOGE
in
MOBILE MILLIONS PART TWO
THE JUNIOR WOODCHUCKS ASKED SCROOGE FOR MONEY TO HELP BUY LAND FOR A NEW HEADQUARTERS. BUT SCROOGE HAS OTHER PROBLEMS— HIS MOLDY MONEY NEEDS SOME FRESH AIR, SO A SPECIAL 'MONEY BIN MOVER' IS TRANSPORTING IT TO THE SEASIDE! UNFORTUNATELY, IT HAS JUST BEEN 'BORROWED' BY THOSE RASCALS, THE BEAGLE BOYS!
THEY'RE TAKING EVERY BIT OF CASH I OWN! DON'T JUST STAND THERE, DONALD! DO SOMETHING!
UM, SURE! ANY IDEAS?
2000-099
HEY, THERE GO OUR UNCLES!
AND WITHOUT THE MONSTER MONEY BIN MOVER! WHAT HAPPENED?
GUYS! OVER HERE!
THE BEAGLE BOYS PULLED A FAST ONE ON UNCLE SCROOGE!
NEVER MIND THAT! WE NEED A FAST CAR!
AND SOON...
THE MONEY-MOVER SURE LEAVES CLEAR TRACKS! WE'LL CATCH UP WITH THEM IN NO TIME!
AND SURELY THEY CAN'T HIDE SOMETHING OF THAT SIZE!
WAK! THEY'RE NOT EVEN TRYING TO HIDE IT!
THE NERVE OF THOSE CROOKS!

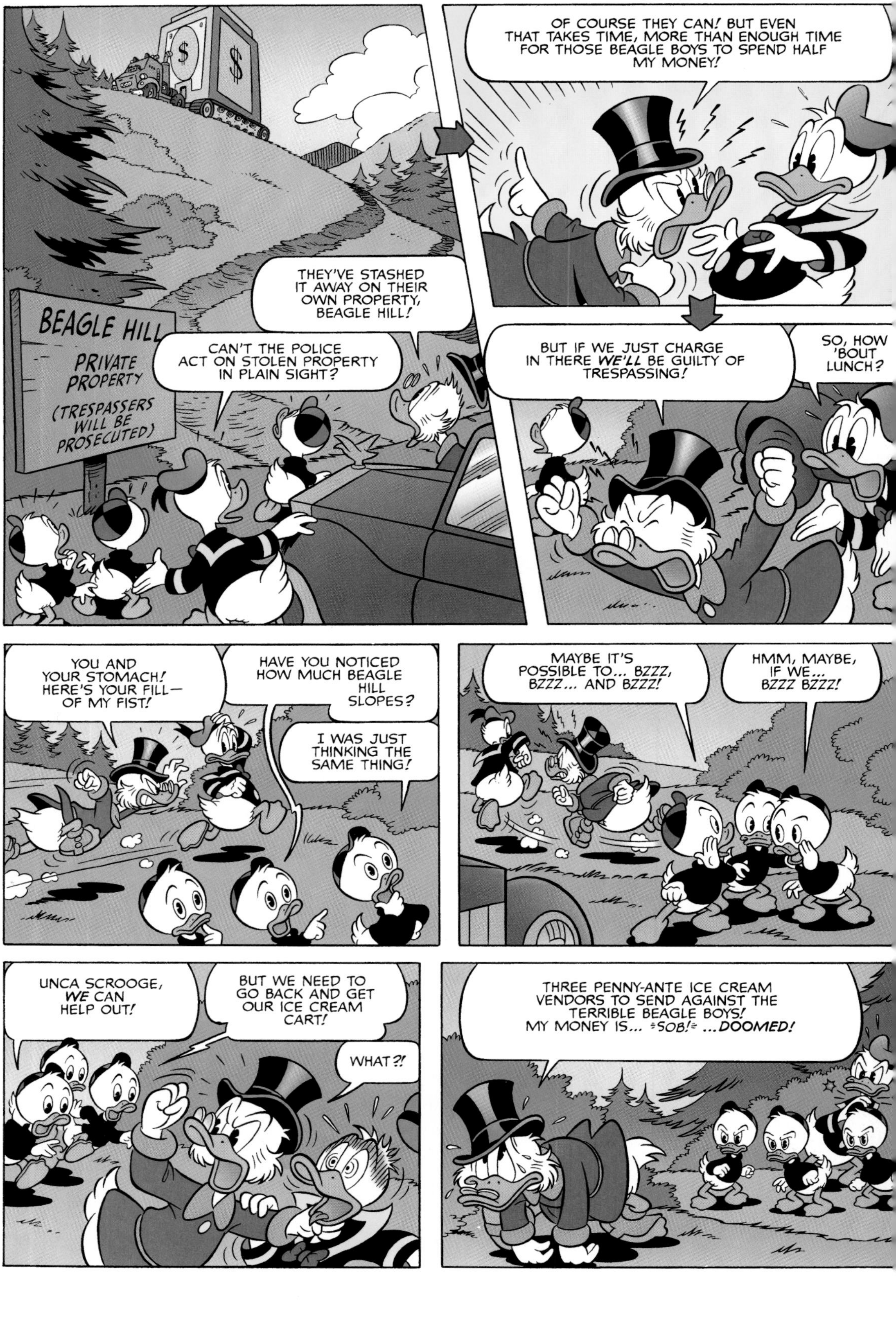
THEY'VE STASHED IT AWAY ON THEIR OWN PROPERTY, BEAGLE HILL!
BEAGLE HILL PRIVATE PROPERTY (TRESPASSERS WILL BE PROSECUTED)
CAN'T THE POLICE ACT ON STOLEN PROPERTY IN PLAIN SIGHT?
OF COURSE THEY CAN! BUT EVEN THAT TAKES TIME, MORE THAN ENOUGH TIME FOR THOSE BEAGLE BOYS TO SPEND HALF MY MONEY!
BUT IF WE JUST CHARGE IN THERE WE'LL BE GUILTY OF TRESPASSING!
SO, HOW 'BOUT LUNCH?
YOU AND YOUR STOMACH! HERE'S YOUR FILL— OF MY FIST!
HAVE YOU NOTICED HOW MUCH BEAGLE HILL SLOPES?
I WAS JUST THINKING THE SAME THING!
MAYBE IT'S POSSIBLE TO... BZZZ, BZZZ... AND BZZZ!
HMM, MAYBE, IF WE... BZZZ BZZZ!
UNCA SCROOGE, WE CAN HELP OUT!
BUT WE NEED TO GO BACK AND GET OUR ICE CREAM CART!
WHAT?!
THREE PENNY-ANTE ICE CREAM VENDORS TO SEND AGAINST THE TERRIBLE BEAGLE BOYS! MY MONEY IS... SOB! ...DOOMED!

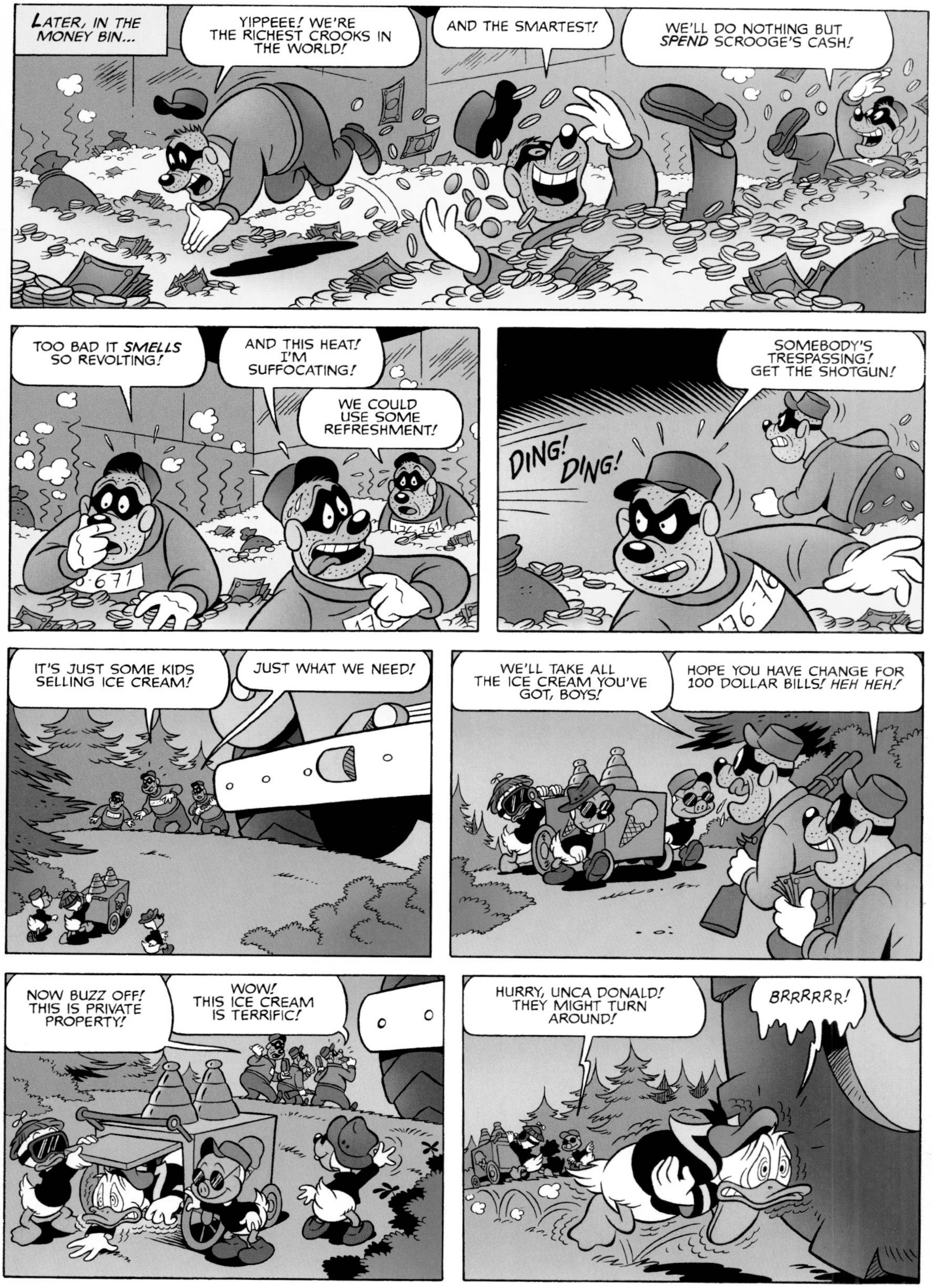

LATER, IN THE MONEY BIN...
YIPPEEE! WE'RE THE RICHEST CROOKS IN THE WORLD!
AND THE SMARTEST!
WE'LL DO NOTHING BUT SPEND SCROOGE'S CASH!
TOO BAD IT SMELLS SO REVOLTING!
AND THIS HEAT! I'M SUFFOCATING!
WE COULD USE SOME REFRESHMENT!
DING! DING!
SOMEBODY'S TRESPASSING! GET THE SHOTGUN!
IT'S JUST SOME KIDS SELLING ICE CREAM!
JUST WHAT WE NEED!
WE'LL TAKE ALL THE ICE CREAM YOU'VE GOT, BOYS!
HOPE YOU HAVE CHANGE FOR 100 DOLLAR BILLS! HEH HEH!
NOW BUZZ OFF! THIS IS PRIVATE PROPERTY!
WOW! THIS ICE CREAM IS TERRIFIC!
HURRY, UNCA DONALD! THEY MIGHT TURN AROUND!
BRRRRRR!

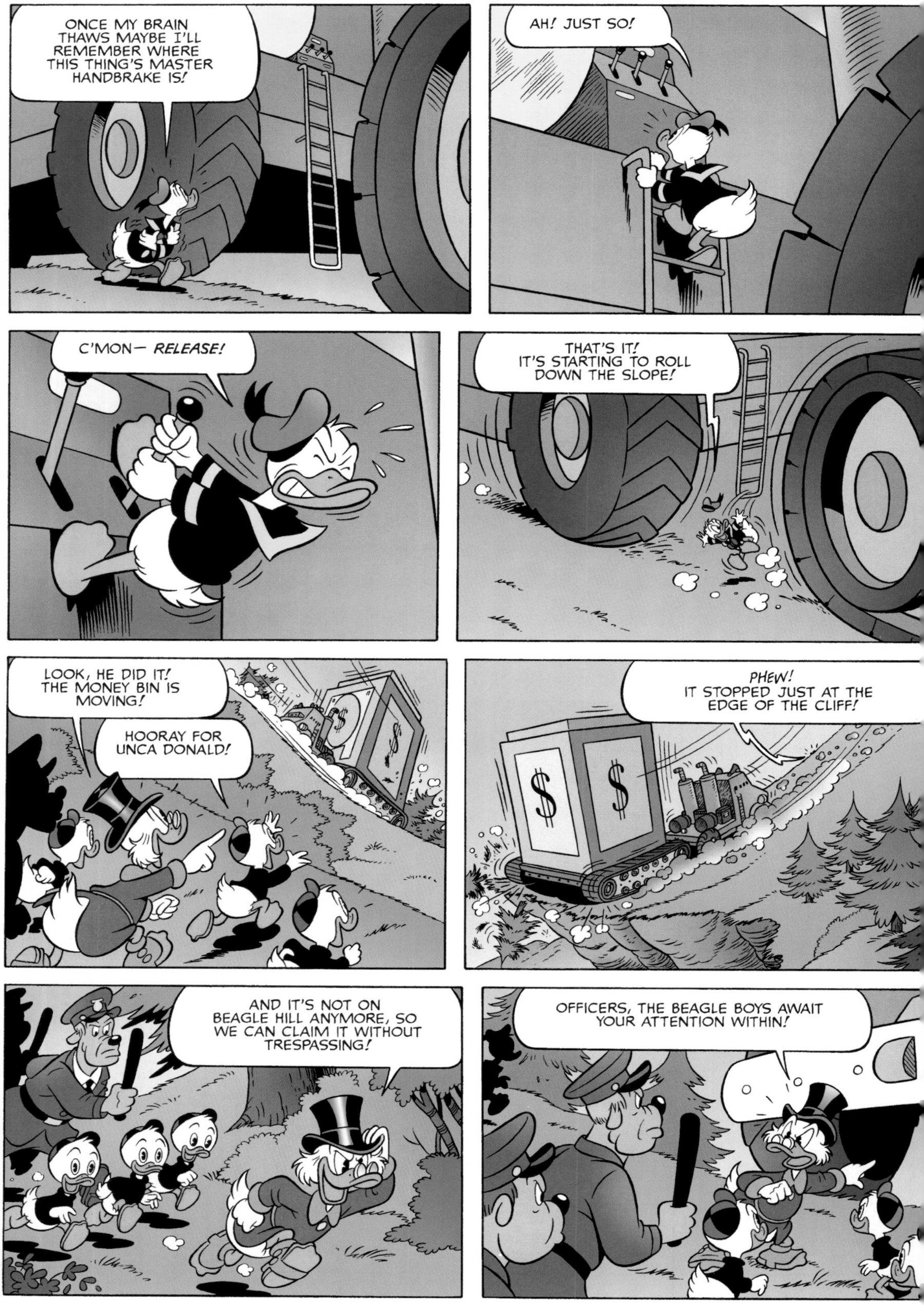
ONCE MY BRAIN THAWS MAYBE I'LL REMEMBER WHERE THIS THING'S MASTER HANDBRAKE IS!
AH! JUST SO!
C'MON— *RELEASE!*
THAT'S IT! IT'S STARTING TO ROLL DOWN THE SLOPE!
LOOK, HE DID IT! THE MONEY BIN IS MOVING!
HOORAY FOR UNCA DONALD!
PHEW! IT STOPPED JUST AT THE EDGE OF THE CLIFF!
AND IT'S NOT ON BEAGLE HILL ANYMORE, SO WE CAN CLAIM IT WITHOUT TRESPASSING!
OFFICERS, THE BEAGLE BOYS AWAIT YOUR ATTENTION WITHIN!

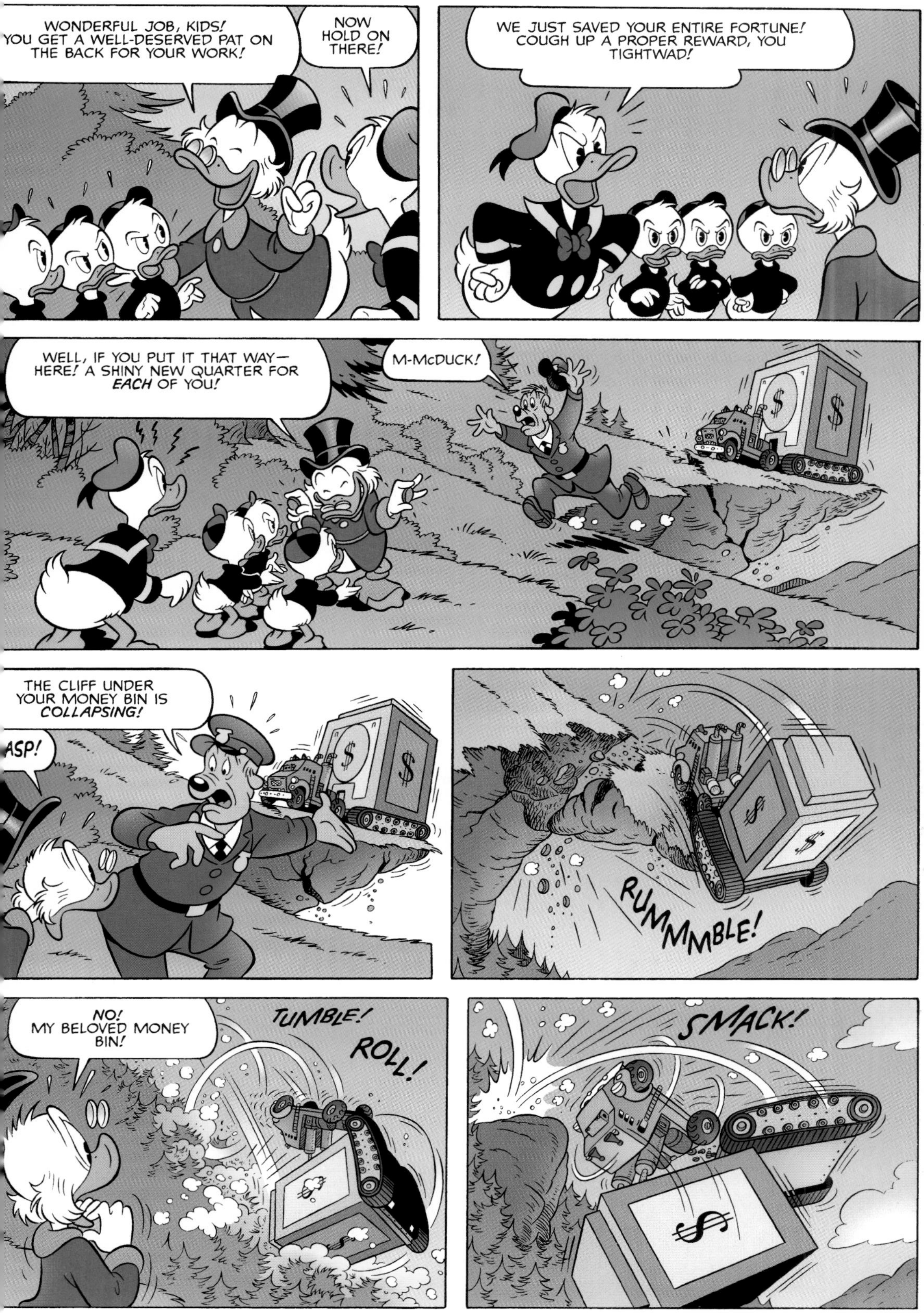
WONDERFUL JOB, KIDS! YOU GET A WELL-DESERVED PAT ON THE BACK FOR YOUR WORK!
NOW HOLD ON THERE!
WE JUST SAVED YOUR ENTIRE FORTUNE! COUGH UP A PROPER REWARD, YOU TIGHTWAD!
WELL, IF YOU PUT IT THAT WAY— HERE! A SHINY NEW QUARTER FOR *EACH* OF YOU!
M-McDUCK!
THE CLIFF UNDER YOUR MONEY BIN IS *COLLAPSING!*
ASP!
RUMMMBLE!
NO! MY BELOVED MONEY BIN!
TUMBLE!
ROLL!
SMACK!

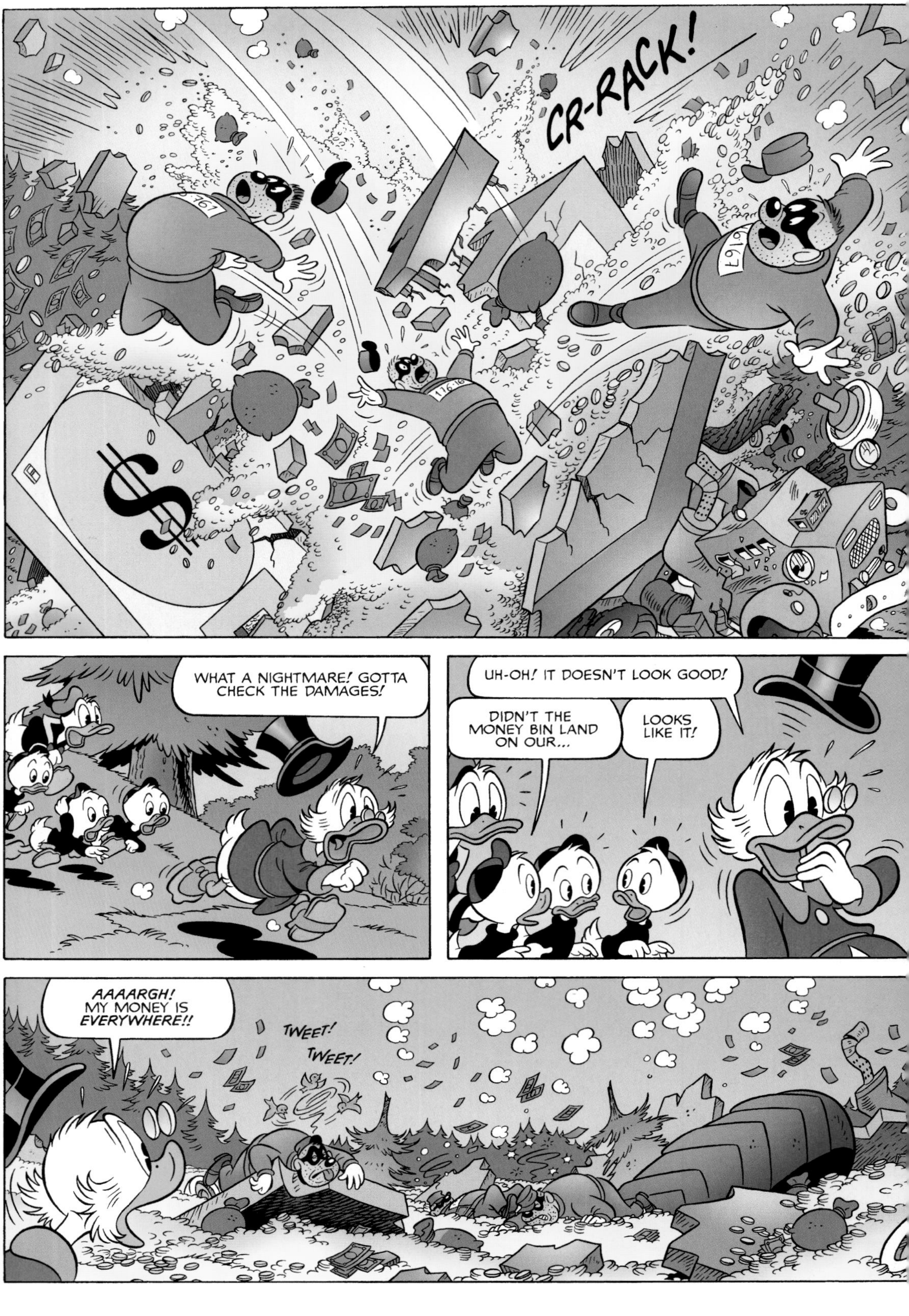
CR-RACK!
WHAT A NIGHTMARE! GOTTA CHECK THE DAMAGES!
UH-OH! IT DOESN'T LOOK GOOD!
DIDN'T THE MONEY BIN LAND ON OUR...
LOOKS LIKE IT!
AAAARGH! MY MONEY IS EVERYWHERE!!
TWEET!
TWEET!

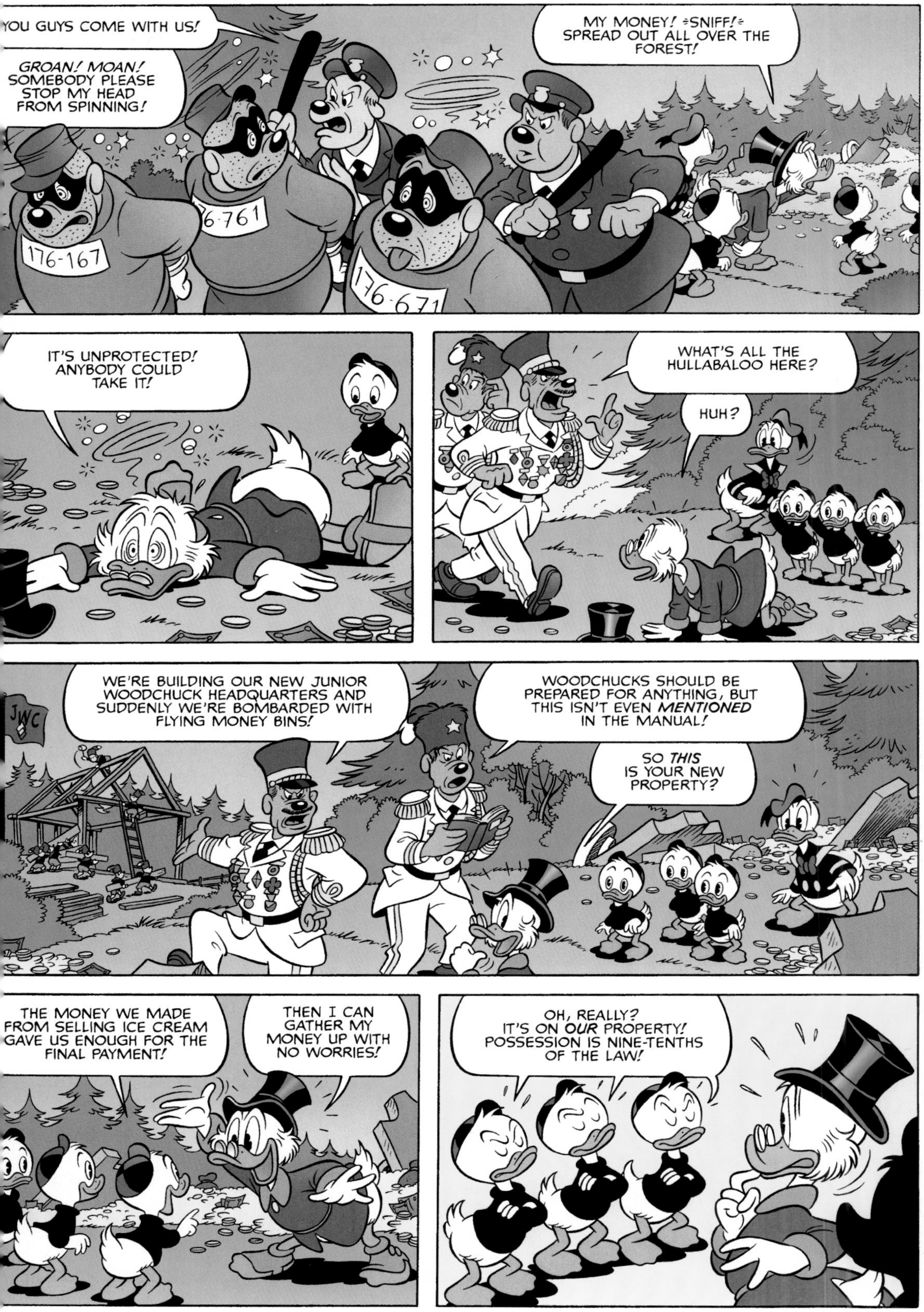
YOU GUYS COME WITH US!
GROAN! MOAN! SOMEBODY PLEASE STOP MY HEAD FROM SPINNING!
176-167
76-761
176-671
MY MONEY! =SNIFF!= SPREAD OUT ALL OVER THE FOREST!
IT'S UNPROTECTED! ANYBODY COULD TAKE IT!
WHAT'S ALL THE HULLABALOO HERE?
HUH?
JWC
WE'RE BUILDING OUR NEW JUNIOR WOODCHUCK HEADQUARTERS AND SUDDENLY WE'RE BOMBARDED WITH FLYING MONEY BINS!
WOODCHUCKS SHOULD BE PREPARED FOR ANYTHING, BUT THIS ISN'T EVEN MENTIONED IN THE MANUAL!
SO THIS IS YOUR NEW PROPERTY?
THE MONEY WE MADE FROM SELLING ICE CREAM GAVE US ENOUGH FOR THE FINAL PAYMENT!
THEN I CAN GATHER MY MONEY UP WITH NO WORRIES!
OH, REALLY? IT'S ON OUR PROPERTY! POSSESSION IS NINE-TENTHS OF THE LAW!

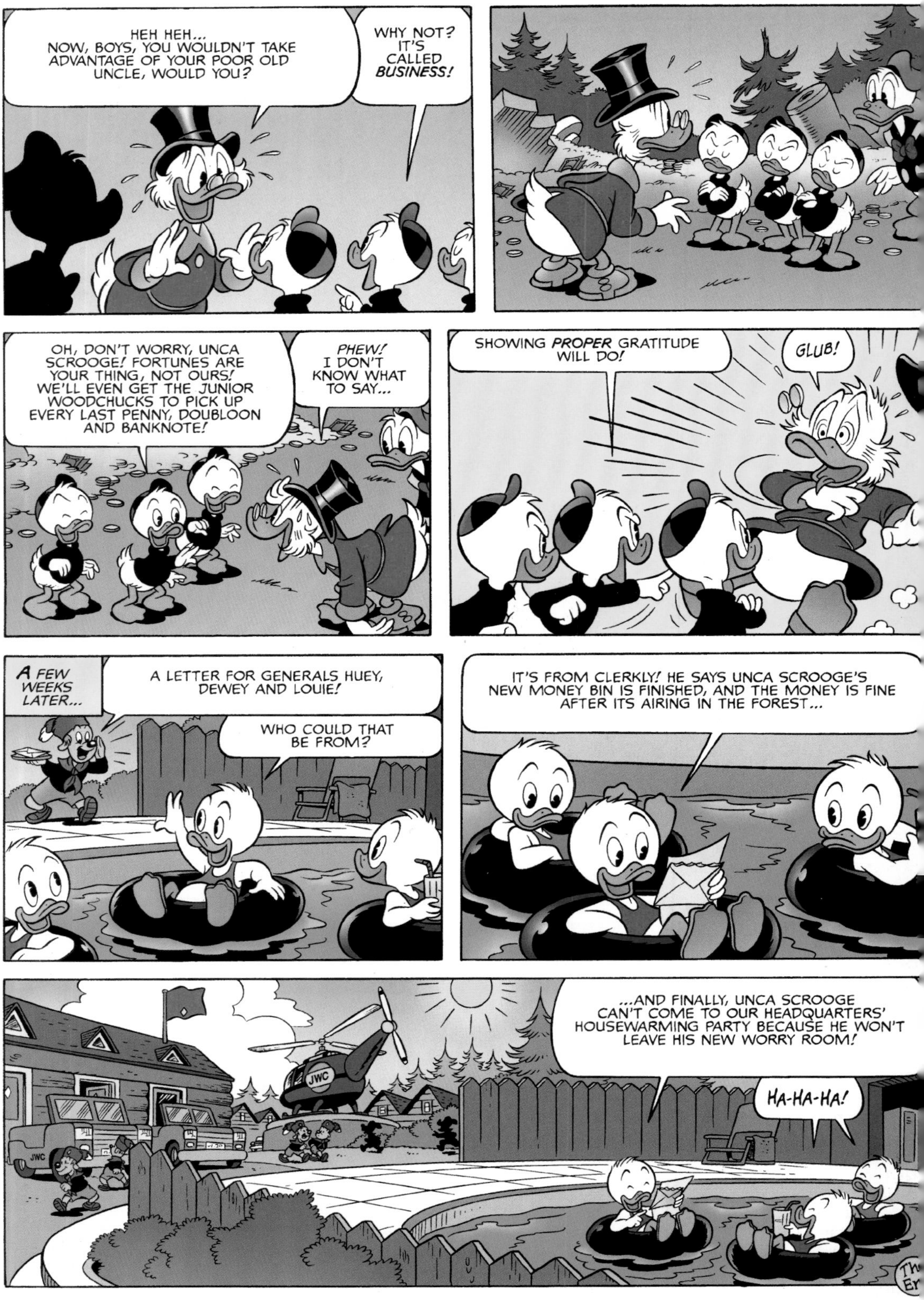
HEH HEH... NOW, BOYS, YOU WOULDN'T TAKE ADVANTAGE OF YOUR POOR OLD UNCLE, WOULD YOU?
WHY NOT? IT'S CALLED *BUSINESS!*
OH, DON'T WORRY, UNCA SCROOGE! FORTUNES ARE YOUR THING, NOT OURS! WE'LL EVEN GET THE JUNIOR WOODCHUCKS TO PICK UP EVERY LAST PENNY, DOUBLOON AND BANKNOTE!
PHEW! I DON'T KNOW WHAT TO SAY...
SHOWING *PROPER* GRATITUDE WILL DO!
GLUB!
A FEW WEEKS LATER...
A LETTER FOR GENERALS HUEY, DEWEY AND LOUIE!
WHO COULD THAT BE FROM?
IT'S FROM CLERKLY! HE SAYS UNCA SCROOGE'S NEW MONEY BIN IS FINISHED, AND THE MONEY IS FINE AFTER ITS AIRING IN THE FOREST...
JWC
...AND FINALLY, UNCA SCROOGE CAN'T COME TO OUR HEADQUARTERS' HOUSEWARMING PARTY BECAUSE HE WON'T LEAVE HIS NEW WORRY ROOM!
HA-HA-HA!